ORIENTAL ANTIQUES AND COLLECTIBLES, A GUIDE

ORIENTAL ANTIQUES AND COLLECTIBLES, A GUIDE

Arthur and Grace Chu

CROWN PUBLISHERS, INC.   NEW YORK

ACKNOWLEDGMENTS

We wish to thank our good friends John T. Ma, Curator, and David Tseng, Deputy Curator, of the Hoover Institution, Far Eastern Division, Stanford University, for valuable assistance in our research; Mr. and Mrs. Henry H. Johnson, whose friendship we have cherished through many years, for technical advice in photography. Mrs. Johnson, head of the Forestry Library at the University of California, Berkeley, was particularly helpful in gathering material for the book.

We are much indebted to Professor Michael Sullivan, Curator, Stanford University Museum, for permission to photograph the outstanding specimens of Oriental art included among our illustrations; the National Palace Museum, Taiwan; the Oakland City Museum, Oakland, California; and the many friends whose contributions are invaluable.

We reserve our special thanks for our editor, Mrs. Kathryn Pinney, whose critical acumen, advice, and genuine interest in the subject constitute a major factor in making this book possible.

CONTENTS

INTRODUCTION

"Why do you collect oriental antiques?"

"My great . . . great uncle captained one of the first clipper ships that went to Canton. He brought back hundreds of oriental objects, but they're all gone now. His diary's still in the family, though—and he wrote that at first there was no money to buy products from China. But then in New England they found a wild root growing which the Chinese believed had a magic rejuvenating power, a root called ginseng. They filled the ships with this root, and the captains used it to barter with the Chinese for porcelain, silk, lacquer. That's how my interest developed, and once you start collecting, of course—you can never stop."

"My grandfather was a consular official in Yokohama during the early 1900s. He traveled all over the Far East—Tokyo, Kyoto, Shanghai, Seoul. I loved to visit him when I was a child because his house was filled with beautiful things he'd brought home. So you see I became interested rather early."

"I must have been an Oriental in my last incarnation."

Besides these sentimental reasons, there is also the factor of investment. You can start with as little money as you can afford, and if you choose and buy wisely, before long you will have a small but valuable collection to enjoy instead of an impersonal bankbook or a pile of stock certificates. As one man proudly said to us, referring to his modest collection, "I never tire of my things. Their value will increase and increase. They're better than money in the bank."

It is much cheaper to collect oriental antiques or art objects than those in almost any other category. For instance, a Tiffany lamp may cost $1,000, and not necessarily be an outstanding piece in spite of the price. But you can, for less than that amount, get a genuine eighteen-inch K'ang-hsi porcelain vase, circa 1700, in vivid powder blue or mirror black, every inch of it classical perfection, or a small vase with the exciting peach-bloom glaze, a gem you will never tire of looking at or holding in your hands.

Another example is porcelain flowers. Some that were made by American ceramists and recently exhibited by a major museum were priced at an average of $2,000 each, but Chinese and Japanese hand-made porcelain flowers and figurines of the finest quality and workmanship can be bought for $50 apiece. There are also the charming Chinese pottery ducks (always dear to the Chinese heart, for the duck is considered a creature of happy and carefree disposition), modeled with loving care, either chewing contentedly on a water-lily stem or emerging from an entanglement of lotus leaves and flowers. We refer, not to those inch-high ducks produced by the millions and sold for a few pennies apiece twenty-five years ago, but to the large and almost life-size ones with thick, unctuous flambé glazes in various shades of brown, green, and peacock blue.

For still another example: A Picasso commands a small or, rather, a large fortune. But for less than $2,000 one can have a Ch'i-Pai-shih (he is the greatest contemporary Chinese artist [1861–1957]). And there will be just as great aesthetic satisfaction from owning it, especially if the buyer is a lover of oriental painting.

It is still comparatively easy to collect oriental objects into which the craftsman has put the extra personal touch that, call it whatever you will, represents the desire to create something original. The time to assemble a modest collection on a moderate budget, for enjoyment *or* profit, is now, but it will not be with us for long. The oriental countries are already either entirely industrialized or in an accelerated process of becoming so. Japan is more interested in making transistor radios and color TV's than in producing hand-crafted objects like their exquisite cloisonnés. China, when she resumes her trade with the West, will not flood the market with handmade items. Even Korea, whose history is a sad record of constant invasion by foreign nations and whose exports in bygone times were negligible, is exporting manufactured goods today.

The terms "Orient" and "oriental," in this book, are used in a broad sense. They refer to China, Korea, and Japan, which actually form one cultural entity. It is difficult to talk about the products of one of these countries without referring to the others. Of the three, China was the pioneer in nearly all the art media. The techniques spread first to Korea and then to Japan. It is interesting to note that the formal dress and coiffure of Japanese women still retain the features of high fashion of the Chinese T'ang dynasty, A.D. 618–907; and Japanese still sit on the floor, an ancient practice that the Chinese gave up many centuries ago. So close-knit are the cultural ties between China, Korea, and Japan that they are very much in evidence to this day.

China has had a continuous culture for 4,000 years. She is one of the largest and certainly the most populous countries in the world, and a large percentage of her tremendous population show an inherent joy in producing art and artistic objects. Her rulers have always been great patrons of the arts—some of the emperors of the Sung and Ming dynasties were themselves noted artists. More recently, during the eighteenth century, Emperor Ch'ien-lung and his descendants were avid collectors, and they gave further impetus to the various arts. The Chinese upper class, the scholar class, has always dabbled in art and art collecting. The whole nation, in fact, developed from the earliest time a profound interest in and respect for things that are artistic and old. This description can also be applied to the Korean and Japanese people.

Today, millions of collectible items in jade, porcelain, bronze, lacquer, and other materials are still in existence. Many of them found their way into the United States after trade began between the East and West. Besides a constant stream of imports from the Orient during the last 200 years, American businessmen, missionaries, and wealthy tourists brought innumerable such items to the New World, some good, some bad. Most of these have become available through estate sales, auctions, antique shops, and even flea markets, whence they have been or are being greedily and indiscriminately snapped up by dealers and collectors.

Contrary to popular belief, the United States is currently a fertile field for hunters of oriental antiques. Many dealers even bought such antiques in America and shipped them to the Far East to supply the demand of well-heeled American and European tourists at Expo-70 in Tokyo. One dealer confided to us, early in 1970, "My whole collection of netsuke is now on its way to Tokyo."

The purpose of this book is to supply basic knowledge for average collectors with limited means but plenty of time to browse around the neighborhood antique shops and flea markets. To these gentle and genial souls who have an appreciation for the old, the exotic, and above all for the things of beauty created and crafted by distant peoples in a by-gone age, the authors would like to dedicate this book. We do not try to be scholarly or exhaustive. If you are an advanced collector, you are no doubt familiar with the many fine books and scholarly articles already in print, and will continue to follow with interest those written in the future to enrich the knowledge of this vast field that still needs research, exploration, and interpretation.

The advanced collector, therefore, will regard this book as the personal opinions and prejudices of two fellow collectors. To the beginner, however, we hope it will become a primer for collecting in the oriental field.

A large part of this book deals with market conditions, and we intend to "tell it like it is." A number of illustrations are provided. Too often, we feel, books on oriental art are inclined to picture the same celebrated museum items over and over again. Ordinary collectors, after all, do not often find nor can they afford pieces of such distinguished quality. Most items illustrated in this book represent specimens a collector can actually find on the market. A few museum articles are included, purely for the purpose of supplying the necessary historical background or to offer an opportunity for making comparisons. The importance of comparison cannot be overstressed. Chinese advanced collectors always advise beginners to "compare, compare, and compare." It must be said that visiting museums and seeing the real things, then comparing them with what the market has to offer, is the only way the collector can develop his ability to distinguish the genuine from the fake, and the artistic from the vulgar.

1

ADVICE FOR THE COLLECTOR

A FRIEND OF OURS IS A WATCHMAKER WHO HAS A SHOP ON THE edge of Chinatown, San Francisco. One day his 78-year-old widowed landlady asked him to help her clean the basement. They found literally hundreds of small, empty Chinese cough syrup and other patent medicine bottles, and since there was no place to dump them, he put them in boxes and left them in the yard. Later, he decided to clean a few and display them among his watches—he has a large display window with plenty of room for knickknacks. That same day a group of tourists came by and stopped before his window. They talked excitedly among themselves, and then they sauntered in.

"What are those little bottles in the window?" a woman asked.

"They're Chinese medicine bottles of one kind or another," he answered.

"Now, tell us the truth," demanded the woman. "Aren't they opium bottles?"

"Honestly, lady," said our friend, "I never saw an opium bottle in my life."

"Come on, young fella!" an old man in the group spoke up. "I was here during the early twenties, and this town was full of opium dens. You could smell opium up and down the street." He opened one bottle and inhaled from it. "Sure, it smells like opium. Look, if this isn't an opium bottle, I'll eat it—I mean smoke it—ha-ha-ha!"

"How much do you want for one?" asked the woman.

"A dollar."

"I'll take them all. Won't they make great gifts for the girls in my collectors' club?"

"Sure, sure! Gen-u-wine opium bottles from Chinatown, San Francisco, 1920 vintage. Maybe even 1890," encouraged the old man.

So our friend took another dozen bottles to the shop, raised the price to $2 each, and sold them all in a week. Eventually, weeks later, the last batch he sold for $5 each. With business booming like that, he no longer had time to clean the bottles (or to repair watches, for that matter). The bottles were snapped up as soon as they appeared in the window, though he was sure that a couple of times customers had read the faintly discernible bilingual labels, "Patent Cough Medicine" and so on, which, however, they manfully ignored.

"I never once told people they were opium bottles." Our friend shrugged. "If they want to think so—what can I do?"

Since collectors are willing to pay almost any price for something they don't have in their collections, dealers profit by their gullibility. For instance, the dealer specializing in snuff bottles keeps on hand a wide selection, which he gets from traveling salesmen, called "pickers" in the trade. They search for salable antiques in every corner of the world. Occasionally they find a snuff bottle they believe will be particularly appealing to collectors, and secretly they send it to an "antique manufacturer" in Hong Kong to be copied. They may order as many as a thousand bottles. These "instant antiques," usually made of ivory but more often of bone, are expertly antiqued. They look authentic on the outside, but the manufacturer has not bothered to shape the bottle on the inside. There is only a straight narrow hole to accommodate the little spoon.

Recently a great many ivory snuff bottles shaped like an old mandarin couple, richly and boldly antiqued with pigment, suddenly appeared on the market. They certainly looked striking and unusual. The first one we saw was in the shop of a dealer who had bought the piece for $100 while on a trip to Honolulu. Three weeks later, the itinerant distributor arrived and started selling the same snuff bottles to dealers for $50 each, then $25, then $10, until the market was flooded.

The dealers were royally gypped, but they had no need to worry. In six months customers had bought all their bottles, and one dealer remarked wistfully, "I wish that the guy who sold me those ivory mandarins would come again."

"You mean—you want to punch his nose?"

"No. I wouldn't mind buying another dozen from him."

Many netsuke collectors can recall the days when, fascinated and intoxicated by the beauty of these ingenious Japanese objects, they bought indiscriminately the genuine as well as the wax and celluloid imitations, complete with the signatures of the supposed carvers. Oftentimes they purchased whole collections of these worthless things with the assurance of the dealer that he had acquired them from a collector, who had bought each one in Japan. One collector told us that, of the several dozens he had purchased during his salad days, nearly one third had proved to be imitations.

On the subject of snuff bottles again: At a recent auction there was a set of six crude ceramic snuff bottles with raised biscuit work, which was haphazardly slapped over with the three-color glazes. The bottles were contained in a small case lined inside with blue silk and covered with a glass cover. They were labeled as Ming, which of course was patent nonsense because snuff was hardly known during the Ming dynasty. Actually, these little bottles were manufactured in great quantities before World War II to satisfy the tremendous demand of Western tourists. They could be bought packaged in silk-lined cases with glass covers in sets of four, six, or eight at all Chinese seaport cities for less than $10. Sometimes peddlers would bring them to the dock, and tourists could buy them without even getting off the ship. The set described above was sold at the auction for $200. At the next sale, the auctioneer appeared with another set of the same type. The owner may have had several hundred sets in his warehouse!

There are black sheep in every profession, and the antique trade is no exception. The following types of salesmanship should immediately put the collector on guard:

1. *The Old Lady Line:* "I bought this from an 85-year-old oriental lady, and she told me her grandfather brought it from the old country in 1845." *Advice:* Ignore the sales pitch.

2. *The Museum Approach:* (*a*) "We took this bowl to the museum, and they authenticated it as Ming. Naturally they couldn't give us a written certificate—you know a museum curator doesn't do *that*." A museum curator, who is of course knowledgeable, does not always have time to appraise things brought to the museum. The dealer may have shown the bowl to an assistant whose job was strictly "public relations." Of course there are talkative docents, though their main duty is to conduct tours, not to appraise items brought by visitors. (*b*) "The X Museum sent their people to look at this Korean bronze Buddha yesterday. They told me they are very interested and might come and buy it this afternoon."

Advice: Tell the dealer you are in no position to compete with a museum. As far as you are concerned, you still think the piece is worth only so much, and that's your final offer.

3. *The Sweet Use of Consignment:* The dealer claims that the piece is on consignment from a very well-known collector whose name he has sworn not to disclose. This anonymous collector bought the piece from the Y gallery—a big outfit known for its absolute honesty. Yes, the owner not only has the sales receipt as proof, but also has had the piece appraised by Mr. So-and-So (Mr. Integrity himself). So you buy it, and the dealer promises to get the papers for you by next Monday. When that day comes, the dealer is most apologetic. The owner must keep the sales receipt for tax purposes, and he can't find the appraiser's certificate. He did try. Right now, though, he has gone to Rome. You see, he's a manufacturer with branch offices all over the world, and he has oodles of money. So you say. "Oh, well—" The piece is no doubt a fake.

Advice: Before you write the check, get the papers or a written guarantee that the papers will be given to you. The former owner has no use for them, and he has no reason to keep them.

4. *The Going-Out-of-Business Routine:* Appealing to the buyer's bargain-hunting instincts, some dealers follow this procedure regularly. There is no bargain in this type of advertised sale. We remember arriving home with a blue and white tea jar bought at a 30 percent discount. Upon removing the price tag we found that the original price, in indelible grease pencil, was still faintly visible. It was 10 percent less than the price we had paid; thus, the dealer had even made his customer help pay for the advertisement.

A final word of caution: Some dealers, even in well-established antique shops, do not have price labels on their wares. We always have the feeling, perhaps unjustified, that they appraise prospective customers and then name a price for any item inquired about. For the smart dealer, this makes a natural opening for a potent sales talk calculated to sweep the unsophisticated buyer off his or her feet.

A collector of modest means should take the time to prepare himself well in the field of his particular interest by reading, researching, and visiting museums. He should always make his own decisions and resist buying anything he doesn't have the haziest knowledge of. And he needs to be wary of all purported "sales." Listening to the advice or expertise of the fellow sitting next to you at an auction, or letting a dealer sway your decision one way or the other, is the worst thing you can do with your money and to yourself.

HOW AND WHERE TO FIND ORIENTAL ANTIQUES

ANTIQUES HAVE BECOME BIG BUSINESS IN THE LAST DECADE. SINCE it is impossible for anyone to know everything about them, both collectors and dealers usually specialize in a specific category. Dealers have the further limitation of having to buy what they can get—and few of them have the time to research every item that comes their way. Therefore a collector who is especially knowledgeable about his category of interest can often get things at a fraction of their value.

Successful antique dealers are temperamentally artistic. Many are collectors themselves, sometimes retired people who have a lifetime of collecting experience behind them. Usually they have time on their hands and enjoy trading anecdotes with customers. The next time you are browsing in your neighborhood antique shop, try to get acquainted. When you get to know a dealer, you can ask him to hold an item for a couple of days while you make up your mind or do some extra research on it. And dealers often give special price reductions to their regular customers.

But be careful. If you notice some treasure in a shop at a fraction of its value, don't look smug or say to the dealer, in effect, "Now here's an item I know more about than you." The unforgettable or unforgivable insult is not the monetary part—dealers are almost always willing to give you a reduced price on an item you fall in love with—at least so they say. What hurts their pride is the recognition that a customer is profiting from their ignorance; like other specialists, they want to be considered experts in their business.

The antique shop, from the small neighborhood "elegant junk" type to the exclusive gallery, should be considered the primary source of supply for the collector. An antique cooperative makes shopping and browsing easier because there are usually several shops under one roof, and often there is an atmosphere of congeniality, with the coffee-pot perking and a place to sit and chat.

Other rewarding places to look for antiques are flea markets. They are much in vogue now, frequented by dealers and sophisticated collectors as well as amateurs. In the San Francisco Bay Area, for instance, at least fifteen of them are usually open on Saturdays and Sundays. New York City has a well-known market held on spring and autumn Sundays, right in town. The whole country, in fact, is alive with flea markets. They can range in size from hundreds of sellers on acres of open ground to a half-dozen sellers in a vacant lot or church basement. They can be regular affairs, or annual events combined with certain local festivals or celebrations. At Niles, a sleepy town in California, an annual event on the day before Labor Day brings out the entire town and draws people from many miles around. In 1971, over 50,000 came to take part in the frontier atmosphere and to buy from the countless stalls, but comparable turnouts are by no means uncommon in other sections of the country.

At the large metropolitan flea markets, many of the sellers come regularly. They have plenty of savvy, and are actually dealers without permanent locations. Occasionally the owner of an antique shop will enter such a market just to get rid of surplus stock at slightly reduced prices. And there are young couples of both the square and hippie types who make their entire living selling at these markets.

Always look carefully amongst the piles of junk that are sometimes displayed by housewives or youngsters who have just cleaned up a basement or attic and brought all the old clothes, bottles, china, and odds and ends to the flea market to make a few dollars. There are often surprises.

At a flea market we attended, one of the sellers, a middle-aged woman, had a pile of old clothes, old shoes, even a couple of worn-out truck tires. But her stock also included two vases. One was of the cheap dime-store variety. The other immediately attracted our attention because it was an eighteenth-century Chinese red flambé about 14 inches tall with exquisite and elusive rich color. We asked her the price. She answered, without showing much interest, "Oh, I'll take 50 cents for it." Such a vase cannot be bought in any antique shop for less than $200.

At another flea market, we discovered a Chinese pottery peach under a heap of wax fruits, plastic flowers, and the like. An intensive search turned up a pomegranate and a tangerine also. The seller asked a quarter apiece for them. We hastily paid him and put the trophies in our sack, feeling a sort of perverse satisfaction. Just the week before, a dealer we know had seen five Chinese pottery fruits of the same type at an auction preview. On the day of the auction, he drove fifteen miles through a blinding rain, found parking five blocks away from the auction studio, walked through the cold winter downpour, sat in the crowded, smoke-filled hall a good part of the day, and got the fruits at $10 each. He kept two for himself, priced the other three at $25 apiece, and sold them in a few days.

Thrift shops operated by churches or charitable organizations often offer good items at very reasonable prices. The donors are generous in contributing their so-called white elephants, things they do not need, but still of some value. Recently the newly rebuilt Saint Mary's Church in San Francisco received hundreds of donations for a fundraising bazaar. There was a beautiful enamel box that the workers were about to mark with a 25¢ or 50¢ tag when another volunteer came along and read the signature. The little box had been made by none other than Carl Fabergé himself, and was worth at least $10,000. The treasure was immediately returned to the donor, who, however, insisted that the church accept it. "It was given to me by my aunt many years ago," the donor explained. "She loved beautiful things and always had such good taste."

Not long ago a young man showed us a 6- by 4-inch mutton-fat jade set in an enamel mirror with the handle broken off. It was exquisitely carved, in high relief, with a spreading pine tree, two Chinese figures, and a pair of cranes. Originally it could have been the head piece of a ju-i scepter or the frontal piece of a jade belt.

When we told him that it was worth $300 to $500 and asked where it had come from, the young man was flabbergasted. "I was looking around in a small thrift shop," he said, "and here was this piece for 35 cents. I liked it, so I bought it. But I thought it was plastic. When I got out of the car at home, it fell on the concrete floor. I was so surprised that it didn't break that I looked at it more closely and decided it might be some kind of carved stone. I thought you'd be able to tell me what it is."

The happiest finds are often made in the most unexpected places. Such sleepers are usually in the ceramic category, particularly in monochromes such as sang de boeuf and the celadons, but sometimes finds are made among old bronzes, jade, or semiprecious stones. Everyone nowadays recognizes cloisonnés and enamels and knows their value, so they usually bear high prices. And, of course, seldom will anyone sell a carved teakwood chair or table for 50 cents.

So if you have a strong back and don't mind walking, spend your Saturdays and Sundays at the flea markets. Also, never pass up stores that sell used furniture, or thrift shops or garage sales, without stopping to have a "look-see." For our part, we have found it quite unproductive to drive up one street and down another seeking the listed garage sales, but a dealer of our acquaintance got two figurines, a jade and a smoky quartz, for 50 cents each at a garage sale in Philadelphia. He kept the jade piece for his own collection. We were delighted to pay him $10 for the quartz one.

A great percentage of antiques are sold at auctions, and there are advantages in buying at such sales. For one thing, important collections and large estates are generally dispersed at auction, and most well-established auction houses have the expertise to appraise the items accurately. Rarely will they carelessly label an imitation as authentic Ming or Sung. Of course it is not always particularly entertaining to sit or stand for hours in a chilly (or overheated) room amid a crowd of poker-faced bidders waiting for some one specific piece to come up for sale. And when the bidding becomes too competitive, the price can go ridiculously high even if the auctioneer does his best to stop it. Often, however, he can't. Here is a story told by a former auctioneer:

"One day a lady came to a preview and fell in love with a cloisonné vase, which was of ordinary quality. She wanted to know how much it was worth. I told her, 'A cloisonné like that will usually go for fifty dollars.' She asked if she could give us fifty dollars and take the vase home with her. I explained that we *had* to sell it publicly, but I politely assured her that if she was willing to pay fifty dollars, she surely would get it.

"Came the day of the auction, and I noticed this lady sitting patiently in the front row. When the vase came up for bidding she immediately bid fifty dollars. I could see the auctioneer's gavel going down. Then suddenly another woman in the back said, 'Sixty.' A bitter competition began. It ended when the first lady got the vase at the unbelievable price of two hundred and fifty dollars. There was nothing we could do. I was really puzzled, and kind of unhappy for her—until she gave me the check. She was the wife of a big electronics manufacturer, and could certainly afford to throw away two hundred and fifty dollars any time she wanted to."

Once when we were sightseeing in Monterey, California, we stopped at an auction house where a preview was going on. There were many oriental items, and in the back of a showcase was a piece of stone labeled "tomb jade" that appeared interesting to us. Not wanting to come back for the auction next day, we left a written bid of $20, and went on to have our barbecue at the beach. Three days later we got a notice to come and pick up our jade, which had been bid in for us at $15. Ours had been the only bid. Nobody else had wanted the piece, though it was an authentic archaic jade Tsung.

Many collectors of our acquaintance occasionally buy antiques through mail order catalogs, trade papers, or magazine advertisements because the prices are often reasonable. We feel strongly that oriental antiques cannot safely be purchased in this way. One reason is that the field is so wide, the variation in quality so tremendous, and the terminology often so confusing that the description in an advertisement is seldom either adequate or reliable. It takes a true expert to be able to say what an item is and how old it is. For instance, 99 percent of the porcelain with the Ch'ien-lung mark is not Ch'ien-lung even if the advertiser bought the piece as Ch'ien-lung and in good faith believes it to be that. Too many imitations have been made through the years. In a word, oriental antiques cannot be bought sight unseen. Even color pictures cannot be trusted.

In most metropolitan areas, the annual or biannual antique show and sale is a combination of show biz and the display of the most valuable antiques the participating dealers can produce. Before the show opens to the public, there is often a brisk trade among the participating dealers themselves. Sometimes a general dealer at a show may have a few oriental pieces priced below the market. Along comes another who specializes in orientalia, and they are snapped up as soon as they are unwrapped. Still, a knowledgeable collector will have the opportunity of getting an item or two that he has been looking for. Also, on the last day of a big show, most dealers will lower prices on some items so that they have less to pack and tote home. This is the time you can make an offer and perhaps get a good discount. In any case, these annual or biannual shows and sales are well worth the nominal entrance charge. Where else can the collector spend a more enjoyable afternoon or evening?

3

THE MYSTIQUE OF BRONZE

IN CHINA, NOTHING ENGENDERS AS MUCH AWE AND RESPECT AS THE bronze vessels of the Shang and Chou dynasties (1766–221 B.C.).

Ancient Chinese historians recorded that the founder of the Hsia dynasty (2197–1766 B.C.) cast nine bronze tripods from the tribute of metals from his nine provincial heads. These nine tripods, considered to be the virtual symbol of a mandate from heaven, were handed down from one dynasty to another, from one ruler to the next, until the last possessor, fearing they would fall into the hands of the insurgents, threw them into the river. Attempts were made to recover them, but they were never found. However, there is no reason to doubt their existence because ancient scholars and historians all testified to it during their own time, when these tripods were still in the hands of the reigning monarchs. One powerful duke, upon requesting to see the tripods, was roundly rebuked for his presumptuousness by the court of Chou.

Other authorities placed the discovery of bronze even earlier—at the time of the legendary Huang-ti (2698 B.C.). They claimed that coins, in the form of knives, were minted by Huang-ti. They drew sketches of these coins and recorded the names of the owners. But in recent times none have been seen.

The discovery of bronze was no doubt a major event in Chinese history. In warfare, which has always been the chief means of determining the fate of a primitive tribe or nation, this new technology constituted the invention of a new weapons system. Instead of having to chip rocks laboriously, they could now cast dagger-axes, swords, and spears by the thousands and equip a large army in a relatively short time. The Shang people (1766–1122 B.C.), the first to exploit bronze on a large scale, no doubt came to power by virtue of this "auspicious metal."

With the invention of bronze, life also took on more sophistication. Bronze vessels made possible more civilized ways and means of preparing food, and laid the foundation for an elaborate system of etiquette and ceremonial rituals, which became an important part of ancient Chinese life. Generally speaking, such vessels are divided into two classes: those with three or four feet (example "ting"), for cooking or warming food or wine; those with ring feet (example "kuei"), for serving. Various other things were also made of bronze: bells, coins, chariot fittings, weapons of war, and even toys. These items served the needs of the royal and noble houses during festival and ceremonial occasions. Bronze vessels were extremely expensive—ancient literature refers to the noble and powerful families as those "who eat from bronze tripods to the music of bronze bells."

The commissioning of each vessel was a major event. Perhaps astrologers had to select the day when the "auspicious metal" would be cast into the desired vessel. Cattle would be slaughtered to propitiate the spirits. Finally, each finished vessel would be inscribed. The inscription (although the earliest version bore no more than the name of the owner), after stating the purpose of commissioning the vessel, usually concluded with the standard prescript, "Generations of my descendants shall forever treasure this vessel."

As time went on, these inscriptions got longer and longer and became veritable documents. Some recorded an entire royal edict to a certain nobleman, and we can assume the vessel was awarded by the ruler as a special favor. Others recorded the boundary lines between the royal house and a fief, or between two feudal lords, in which cases we can assume that two identical vessels were cast and inscribed with the same document, each party holding one as testimony to the covenant. At times the ruler was likely to give a little royal admonition, such as "Be diligent in your office—avoid excessive drinking." *

These recently discovered documents are a great aid in researching and understanding ancient history. Unlike Westerners, who judge bronzes by their beauty of shape and form, Chinese collectors value

* Inscription on the ting of the Duke of Mao, in the National Palace Museum, Taiwan.

most those with long inscriptions. They are living history to the Chinese, who can also appreciate the beauty of the ancient script.

When a nobleman died, at least some of his vessels were entombed with him and remained there until unearthed by accident, since the intentional disturbing of any grave was always a capital crime. But when the Chinese started building railroads in the early 1900s, many of the ancient tombs were accidentally opened, giving the world the most magnificent specimens of Chinese archaic bronze.

One may ask: Were there not hundreds and thousands of these bronzes in use above the ground? What happened to them? The answer is that in the year 221 B.C. an egomaniac unified China and established the Ch'in dynasty. He crowned himself The First Emperor, and wanted his descendants to rule up to 10,000 generations—meaning forever. He built or, rather, completed the Great Wall. In order to wipe out all history before his own time, he burned books and buried scholars alive. And he collected all the bronze vessels and weapons, melted them down, and recast the metal into twelve giant bronze statues. His dynasty lasted only fourteen years, with two rulers. The bronze giants were melted down by the later rulers and recast into vessels, coins, and weapons.

1. Small bronze items. *Top*: coin, Chou dynasty. *Middle*: percussion instrument, Han or later. *Bottom*: Buddhist plaque, marked the sixth year of Tien-ho, or ca. A.D. 560.

2. Back of a Han dynasty mirror.

The earliest specimens of bronze vessels so far unearthed are of the Shang dynasty (1766–1122 B.C.). Examples from two known sites show that they had already attained a high degree of perfection and stylization. Since the casting technique could not have reached this advanced state all of a sudden, there must have been a long period of experimentation; future excavations may provide scholars with more information about the development of the process. However, the craftsmanship and quality of bronze work began to decline during the Han dynasty (207 B.C.–A.D. 220), perhaps due to the discovery of cheaper and more versatile metals such as iron, and to the technique of mass-producing protoporcelain vessels for everyday use.

We usually think of bronze as an alloy of a fixed amount of copper and tin. Actually, the ancient Chinese knew how to vary the proportions to give the desired color and hardness to the finished product. Of course traces of other metals and impurities often got in accidentally. For instance, iron betrays its presence by a rusty red color in the predominantly blue, green, black, or gray patina. The color of the patina usually depends on the proportion of the metals in the alloy and the mineral content of the earth in which the bronzes were buried. After

3. TLV design (parts of the design look like those letters of the alphabet) on the back of a mirror; quatrefoil around the knob. Han or later.

4. Front of the mirror pictured in illustration 3, showing heavy encrustation.

a millennium or two, the patina becomes a semimetallic substance, which is the indication of age. It has a unique beauty of its own, and should never be entirely removed. Many Westerners like to polish old bronze pieces until they shine like brass. This is a pity. Chinese collectors merely remove the outermost blue green layer, perhaps because of their belief that the blue green substance is poisonous. They often hand-rub the pieces until they show a satiny luster.

Bronzes of great antiquity are rare. However, they can be purchased at a price—a small fortune. If a collector is willing to spend such a large sum of money, how can he be certain that a piece is a genuine Shang or Chou bronze?

The surest way is to have been or, better yet, to be in China and see a peasant by accident uncover an ancient tomb and find several pieces of bronze, and to buy them immediately from his hands. (If they were not gotten from him, the farmer would probably melt them down to make hoes!) After cleaning, and studying the designs, styles, and inscriptions (if any), the collector could arrive at an unmistakable conclusion as to the age of the pieces.

Around 1900 when the railroads were built, more specimens of archaic bronzes from ancient tombs came to light than during any other period of history. Because of the high price paid by antique collectors, particularly wealthy Westerners who sent agents to China to collect for them, there was considerable clandestine robbing of ancient tombs, although down to the time of the Manchu dynasty, which was overthrown in 1912, disturbing graves remained a capital crime. After the last monarchy was overthrown, the rule of the new republic was ineffective. The country was controlled piecemeal by bandits and by warlords who were no better than bandits. Both found themselves unable to resist the highly lucrative enterprise of hunting for buried treasures. They worked at night because this type of activity was still much abhorred and despised by the Chinese. When a cache of treasure was unearthed, it was immediately sold to the waiting agents. The warlords would use the money to buy guns and ammunition, often through the same agency, to equip and enlarge their private armies. One General Sun was such an inveterate grave-robber that he was roundly denounced in public by his fellow warlords, who were not averse to such moonlighting jobs of their own.

Naturally, the ideal time to buy a bronze piece was as soon as it was unearthed; otherwise the piece might change hands many times. Today, every effort should be made to trace a vessel to its source, as far back as possible, sifting facts from fiction. This should be the guiding

5. Bronze vessel inlaid with silver in a design of four-clawed dragons and coin with the Chinese characters "Peace in the World." Signed Shih-siu (see inset at lower right), a famous Ming dynasty artist-monk. This beautiful copy may be either Chinese or Japanese. Ca. nineteenth century.

rule of every astute collector, not only of archaic bronzes but of other kinds of antiques as well. Every piece of evidence—affidavits of former owners, appraisers' statements, and the like—should be examined carefully and its reliability tested.

If the seller agrees, by all means take the bronze to a specialist or to a laboratory specializing in testing archaic metals. Modern scientific methods (chemical analysis of the patina and other kinds of tests) can date a piece to within a few hundred years of the time it was cast. The testing procedure takes time and money, but it is certainly worthwhile when buying a piece priced in the hundreds, even thousands, of dollars.

Sometimes, alas, one has to make a quick decision or lose the opportunity to buy a particular piece. But if you are a lover of archaic bronze, you must already have done your homework—read most of the books and articles on the subject, visited museums and spent many hours familiarizing yourself with the different specimens, learned to recognize them by sight. You are also well acquainted with the designs of the various periods (Shang; early, middle, and late Chou) and the styles (pre-Anyang, An-yang, Huai, Shou-Chou, etc.). You may even be able to read the inscriptions and to distinguish the styles of the

6. Coin sword, hung at the door to ward off evil spirits; made of about 150 Chinese coins.

7. Altar set—pair of candlesticks and incense burner.

8. Set of miniature ancient weapons often used in the shrine of the God of War—the Great Warrior Kuan Yü of the Three Kingdoms (A.D. 221–280).

scripts of different periods. If so, you are well equipped to decide to buy the vessel.

If you are not so well prepared, certainly reading this short chapter will not qualify you to pay thousands of dollars for a specimen of archaic bronze. The only sensible thing to do is to wait until you can get the advice of an expert. However, if you have fallen in love with the piece and cannot bear to lose it—and you can afford to take the risk that you may be throwing away a few hundred dollars (assuming that's the price tag)—go ahead, after satisfying yourself on the following points (then, even if the object proves to be a copy, it will still be worth something):

1. Pick up the piece. It should be reasonably heavy. Remember, bronze is relatively soft and can be easily damaged and dented if it is thin. If the ancient wanted his sons and grandsons to treasure and use it forever, it was his duty to make it heavy and thick.

2. It should be covered with patina. Discard anything that looks brassy and shiny.

3. Scrape the patina with your fingernail or, better still, with something harder. See that the patina will not come off easily. Watch out for simulated patina such as paint or material of a greasy consistency.

These tests should be made without fail before purchasing. Of course every collector has his pet method of determining the age or authenticity of archaic bronze. At a recent auction preview of "an important collection of oriental antique treasures," three bronzes purported to be of the Chou dynasty were displayed in locked glass cases, among other valuable things. Covered by a green and blue patina with rusty red spots, they showed great strength of form. The designs were executed with clear-cut smoothness, but unfortunately were betrayed by a confusion of archaic motifs typical of the seventeenth or eighteenth century. The only conclusion a knowledgeable collector could make was that they might be two or three hundred years old, but not the two thousand years stated in the auction catalogue.

Along came an old Chinese gentleman. He summoned the auctioneer and demanded to have the bronzes taken out of the case for examination. Slowly and repeatedly the old man rubbed the first piece with the palm of his hand. Then he closed his eyes and inhaled from his palm deeply and noisily. Sadly and disapprovingly he shook his head. He gave the second object the same treatment, and again shook his head. Then the third. Finally he shuffled away, still shaking his head.

The auctioneer and his five or six eager young assistants had all gathered around, watching unblinkingly. After the old man was gone, they immediately pounced upon the bronzes and rubbed them, closing their eyes and inhaling loudly; then they shrugged their shoulders in bewilderment.

Bronze patina has a sharp acrid smell, particularly if it is relatively new. Like a bloodhound, perhaps, the old man had developed the faculty of smelling out the genuine pieces. His method may not be scientific, but he had, all the same, arrived at the correct conclusion—namely, the vessels were not of as great antiquity as the catalogue claimed.

Even though bronze work as an art form passed its peak of glory around the first century A.D., vessels of bronze continued to be manufactured to satisfy the great demands of ceremonial functions down to more recent centuries. Many of them are heavy, quality objects, and unlike modern imitation pieces, they are certainly worth collecting. After the introduction of Buddhism between the first and second centuries A.D., a great number of Buddhist statuettes, incense burners, and altarpieces, most of them heavily gilded, were cast. Some of the statuettes were molded with great sensitivity and beauty, and the incense burners achieved classic simplicity of form and elegance.

During the neoclassical period of Hsüan-tê, of the Ming dynasty (1426–1435), there was a revival of enthusiasm for bronze work, particularly in tripod incense burners. For this reason, nearly all incense burners made since then, even the crudest ones, bear the reign mark of Hsüan-tê. It must be stressed that reign marks should never be taken seriously. In the eighteenth century, particularly during the long and prosperous reign of the art-loving Emperor Ch'ien-lung (1736–1795), many bronze vessels of the archaic types were cast, some with lavish gold and silver inlays. (Inlaid bronzes began as early as the late Chou period.) They are usually of extremely good quality, and are certainly worth collecting.

To quite another class, however, belong the varieties we must call imitations or even, less complimentarily, fakes. They fall into three groups: (1) those that, immediately after casting, were buried in the ground or immersed in chemicals to develop a respectable patina, which is usually very thin and can be rubbed off; (2) those on which a simulated patina was created with green, blue, or black paint or lacquer, which can also be removed; (3) those with a patina made of an enamel-type material applied heavily over a thin copper base, and with facsimiles of genuine archaic inscriptions then pressed into the coating. Unless the reddish copper base shows through a chipped or dam-

9. Vase of modern white bronze (an alloy with a high percentage of tin or zinc), with archaic motif.

10. Bronze water kettle with enameled repoussé decoration. Export ware.

11. Large Japanese bronze urn with Japanese motif (height 16″, diameter 18″). Probably eighteenth century.

12. Candlestick. The crane stands on a turtle; both are symbols of longevity in Chinese and Japanese mythology. The Japanese turtle has long spreading tail.

aged spot on a piece of this third group, or a powerful magnifying glass reveals that the patina is of imitation material, one can easily be fooled.

There is also a class of bronze of Japanese origin made during the early 1900s. Usually the very large and handsome pieces are of good quality, protected—or, rather, "antiqued"—with a coat of dark brown lacquer. In form and design they can be termed pseudoarchaic Chinese, since they generally show misrepresentations of a medley of archaic motifs. Some carry inscriptions taken directly from genuine pieces, but it is amusing to note how often the inscriptions were put on the wrong vessel. For instance, a wine container, "hu," may carry the inscription: "I made this precious ting." A ting is, of course, a tripod for cooking meat.

13. Japanese bronze vase, ca. 1880, using archaic Chinese motifs, which were often misinterpreted. Note the small refined vase with naturalistic designs, at the left.

14. Japanese bronze vase using archaic Chinese motifs.

15. Japanese bronze vase using archaic Chinese motifs.

People often ask: "Can I, without spending too much money, get a genuine Chinese bronze, no matter how small, but at least two or three hundred years old?"

The answer is, "You can." For twenty-five cents you can go to any antique shop and buy an old Chinese coin, one of those round bronze disks with a square hole in the middle. You can find a Ch'ien-lung (1736–1795) coin in almost any shop. A K'ang-hsi (1662–1722) takes perhaps a day to find, and a Shun-chih (1644–1661) a day or two. Once we found a Sung dynasty coin, circa 1025, for ten cents.

16. Modern Japanese vase painted with gold lacquer. The magnolia flowers are silver plated.

One of the major reasons for the steady decline of Chinese bronze art (except for occasional revivals such as the Hsüan-tê period of the Ming dynasty and the eighteenth century) was the belief that the Shang and Chou masterpieces could not be excelled. Those "sacred vessels," enhanced by their beautiful jadelike patina that took two or three thousand years to form, could hold one spellbound. Even the thought of improving on their design and shape was dismissed as not only superfluous but sacrilegious indeed. This left the Chinese no other avenue but the sterile copying of old pieces.

Japanese bronzes are smooth and of good quality and workmanship, and they are not only available but quite reasonably priced. Collectors of modest means need not spend a great deal and will always get their money's worth. And, since Japanese bronzes as a rule are not extremely old, the question of authenticity does not always come up. The general standards a collector needs to apply are based on the quality and workmanship.

It is reasonable to assume that the Japanese learned the casting technique from the Koreans, who in turn had learned it from the Chinese. The Koreans had long been casting bronze vessels, mirrors, statues in the Chinese tradition, but their methods and techniques were

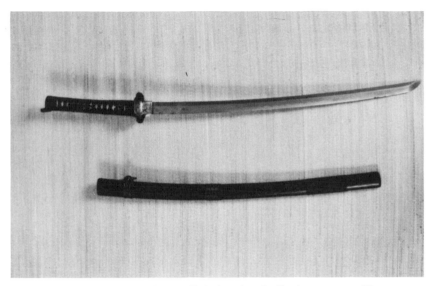

17. The Japanese sword is a well-designed and effective weapon. However, collectors are more interested in the fancy sword guards (tsuba) and other sword ornaments.

so much like those of the Chinese that it would be redundant to elaborate further.

To the Japanese, bronze is not "the auspicious metal" but just one of the many mediums for artistic expression. In fact, the workmen engaged in making the unique wrought-iron kettles used for the tea ceremony and the expensive swords for the samurai may have enjoyed more prestige than the bronze founders. However, after a period of apprenticeship in casting mirrors, Buddhist statues, and the like in the Sino-Korean tradition, the Japanese began to find their own expression. They experimented with bronze alloys to find the best color to suit their purpose. Besides the old Chinese techniques such as inlay and engraving, the Japanese developed many other ways of decorating their bronzes and proved themselves to be very adept at these. Their products range from ojime and tsuba (these have become special fields for collectors and therefore very expensive), statuettes, vases, and urns of a great variety of shapes and forms, to temple lanterns and pagodalike urns and incense burners well over six feet in height and made up of several sections. Their best works are truly examples of elegance, but their worst are overloaded with such an exuberance of decoration that one can easily get caught on the claws of the many entwining dragons.

18. Sword guard, iron, with pierced design of four-petal flowers. *Dr. and Mrs. Marvin Hockabout Collection*

19. Sword guard, iron, decorated with a pierced and foliated square. *Dr. and Mrs. Marvin Hockabout Collection*

20. Iron sword guard with pierced wave pattern. *Dr. and Mrs. Marvin Hockabout Collection*

21. Bronze sword guard decorated with two puppies with gold eyes and a butterfly in gold. Flowers have shakudo (copper alloy with traces of gold) foliage and silver blossoms. *Dr. and Mrs. Marvin Hockabout Collection*

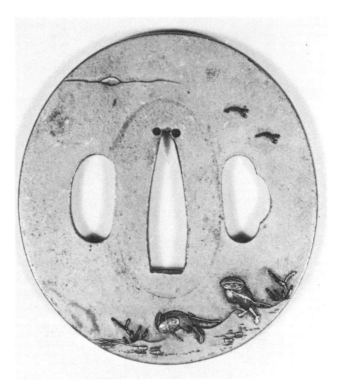

22. This sword guard is decorated with two boatmen in gold hats, pulling on silver ropes. Above is a silver moon. *Dr. and Mrs. Marvin Hockabout Collection*

23. Iron sword guard of irregular squarish shape with three-clawed archaic dragon design. *Dr. and Mrs. Marvin Hockabout Collection*

24. Collar and pommel set (fuchi-kashira). The design of shells and waves is in silver and gold on shakudo ground. *Dr. and Mrs. Marvin Hockabout Collection*

25. Collar and pommel set with shakudo ground. Pommel has flying bird in gold. Collar is decorated with tracery of leaves and water in a single line with gold drops. *Dr. and Mrs. Marvin Hockabout Collection*

26. Collar and pommel set with shakudo ground, signed Masatoshi. The motif is a baton with gold cord. *Dr. and Mrs. Marvin Hockabout Collection*

4

JADE AND OTHER STONES

ALTHOUGH WESTERNERS CONSIDER "CHINA" SYNONYMOUS WITH PORCE-lain, the Chinese themselves would much prefer to be identified with jade, the stone believed to possess all the cardinal virtues and, when carried, to help man remind himself of these virtues. Confucius praised it lavishly, saying that jade shines like benevolence; that it is strong and dependable like wisdom; that, like justice, its edges are sharp but do not cut; that, like truth, it does not hide its flaws. . . .

In ancient times, jade was valued so highly that one prince would offer another several populous cities in trade for a "pi," a piece of circular jade. Kings carried jade at important state functions, and dukes, marquises, and counts bore it in different sizes and shapes as an insignia of their rank. One story has it that these rare jade pieces were made at the court and given to the various feudal lords, and that they conformed to a certain thickness, which was a state secret. In a feudal society, the noblemen were stationed in different parts of the country; the king and his courtiers seldom saw them and therefore would not be able to recognize them. At royal audiences, each jade piece of the nobility was checked through a slot in a master jade piece for verification, before the person was admitted to the court, thus preventing any would-be assassin from masquerading as a nobleman to do harm to the royal person. On the other hand, when the king dispatched a messenger to a far corner of his country to give instructions to a certain feudal lord, the messenger was often provided with a jade piece as a credential.

27. Jade pagoda from the Oakland Museum. This is certainly not a specimen for the collector. To transform an 18,000-pound apple-green jadeite boulder into this 51-inch-high, seven-storied pagoda would take a master carver 1,500 years. Actually, 150 of China's most skilled jade workers labored ten years under the personal direction of the late jade connoisseur Dr. Chang Wen Ti, whose family donated the world-famous treasure to the Oakland Museum in Oakland, California, where it now has its permanent home. Nothing like it was ever made before, nor probably ever will be again. Jade lovers should not miss seeing this testimonial to the ingenuity and patience of Chinese jade carvers.

Each type of jade indicated a certain message, and the bearer could not change it. When the feudal lord saw the jade, he could tell right away whether his king was pleased or displeased with him, and whether he was promoted or fired!

Western experts say that China has produced no jade. History, however, records the following story: A jade expert by the name of Ho once found a boulder in which he believed there was beautiful jade. He presented it to the king. But the king's jade carver, after examining the boulder, said that there could be no jade in it. The enraged king thereupon punished Ho by cutting off his left foot for daring to attempt to cheat him. When a new monarch ascended the throne, Ho again took the boulder to the palace. The new ruler sent for his jade man, and again the verdict was that there was no jade in the boulder. As punishment, Ho lost his right foot. But so strong was his faith that when the third king succeeded the second, Ho asked his family to carry him with the boulder to the throne. The third ruler sent for his jade carver, who happened to be a much more knowledgeable man than his predecessors. He confirmed that there was indeed a piece of beautiful jade in the boulder. To this day, the jade of Ho is proverbially the most beautiful jade known in history. The Chinese like to tell the story, not so much to prove that China indeed shares the honor of being a producer of jade (that may well be true; however, continuous demand exhausted the supply long ago), but to imply the moral that very few people can recognize good jade—or great talent, for that matter.

Indeed, it is extremely difficult to recognize jade, and even the Chinese could be fooled en masse. For instance, not many years ago when chrysoprase from Australia was sold as jade on the oriental market, many Chinese accepted it as genuine and gave it the name "Australian jade," until science proved it otherwise.

Scientifically, jade is either nephrite or jadeite. The old Chinese jades are almost all nephrite. After the seventeenth century, Burma jade (a jadeite) began to be imported into China through the border province of Yunnan. The Chinese, for the purpose of differentiating it from the jade they had always known, gave it the name Fei Ts'ui, or kingfisher green, because of its brilliant green color.

Jade, both nephrite and jadeite, has two outstanding qualities: hardness and toughness. On the Mohs scale, nephrite gives a hardness measure of 6 to 6.5, and jadeite, 6.5 to 7. A steel knife, for instance, will not scratch a piece of jade. Therefore, a jade buyer can easily make his first test by using his pocket knife to scratch the stone (with the permission of the seller, of course). "Scratching" is not merely passing the knife lightly over the jade. The proper procedure is to press the blade tip very hard against the stone and pull it in one direction at least a quarter of an inch, until either a white or a black mark shows. (Choose an area on the bottom of the piece to test; if the stone can be scratched, the test will not ruin its appearance.) If a white mark shows, the knife has scratched the stone, and it is too soft to be jade. If a black mark shows, the stone has scratched the steel blade. Such a stone may be jade, but not necessarily. There are five or six kinds of stone as

28. White jade boulder carved into a landscape with figures. *Stanford University Museum*

29. Water buffalo of yellowish jade with brown spots. *Stanford University Museum*

hard as jade and looking deceptively like it too. For example, idocrase, chrysoprase, and aventurine. Other more complicated tests must follow. But the simple scratch test can help the collector eliminate the softest and cheapest varieties of pseudo jade, such as serpentine and soapstone. These soft stones are often contemptuously referred to in China as "Soochow jade." We were once amazed to hear a dealer explaining confidently to a customer: "This is Soochow jade. It is one of the best jades you can buy." There is a world of difference between jade and "Soochow jade"!

The term "Soochow jade" comes from the scenic and culture-loving town of Soochow, where the people are notoriously soft. When challenged to a fight, a Soochownese would, while beating a hasty retreat to avoid a confrontation, glare at his challenger and say, "It will degrade me to fight a louse like you. I'll go home and get my younger brother to beat you up." This quality is certainly not represented by the tough and hard genuine jade.

If the price asked for a piece of jade is high, it is always wise to take the stone—with the agreement of the seller—to a laboratory where its hardness, specific gravity, and chemical composition can be tested. However, this is a laborious and expensive process, and so anyone who decides to collect jade objects should, besides putting all his five senses to work, try to develop a sixth sense by rubbing and feeling the jades, as the Chinese do. Eventually he will be able to identify genuine jade about 85 percent of the time. That's a pretty good score, one that will rank him in the company of experts.

There are people who claim that if the stone feels cold, then it is jade, or that water dripped onto a piece of jade will immediately run off. These bits of advice are at best misleading. Water will not stay on any highly polished surface. And just how cold is cold?

A more reliable method of identification is to examine the stone under a pocket magnifying glass. A nephrite will reveal, even if only faintly, a fibrous structure; a jadeite shows a mass of interlocking granular or crystalline elements. If the stone (nephrite or jadeite) shows fractures—veins, as people often call them—they should appear splintery and never conchoidal (like a broken shell). Except for gem-quality jade, which can attain a perfect polish, most large specimens contain some inclusions that result in undercutting; that is, in grinding and polishing, the softer material included in the jade will wear off much more than the jade will. Under a magnifying glass, this undercutting shows as a lemon- or orange-rind look.

Because of its unique, closely matted structure, jade is tough. Jade

30. Intricately carved white jade teapot. *Stanford University Museum*

pebbles found in nature or, for that matter, carved jade objects that are round and thick in shape are practically indestructible. That is the reason why so many jade objects carved two or even five hundred years ago are still in circulation today. Unfortunately, this tough quality cannot be easily tested because no one would use a hammer on a piece of beautiful jade. And anyone who wants to prospect for jade should be warned not to swing the hammer too freely at an outcropping. The hammer may bounce back and hit him instead.

Although jade is almost indestructible, it is easily stained, so watch out for dyed jade. A brilliant jade ring that sells for a high price may fade in half a year. Archaic jade objects found in tombs have often changed color and become calcified because chemicals in the soil can transform their appearance.

Westerners prefer the term "tomb jade," rather than "archaic jade." Many of the ancient pieces do come from tombs, but not all. The prices of these artifacts are, shall we say, deservedly high for genuine items because not only are they jade, but jade with the added mystique of having been treasured and fondled by people who lived a millennium or two ago, perhaps kings and princes, who alone could afford them.

In China during the old days the collector could spend a pleasant afternoon in the temple of the City God, the equivalent of our flea market, looking for antiques or artifacts while leisurely nibbling freshly roasted peanuts or other tidbits. Nearly every stand had a few pieces of old jade for sale; some had basketfuls of them. One could pick out any piece that caught his fancy, a cicada that dated back to the first century, or an ornamental piece such as a belt hook, or an archer's ring that might have belonged to an ancient general described in the famous tale "The Romance of the Three Kingdoms."

The seller might haggle with the buyer, but finally he would let the piece go for a couple of dollars.

A collector with more money to spend could drop in at the curio shops, which were situated around the temple for the convenience of collectors, and pick up some larger pieces for five or ten dollars each. He might end up with five or six pieces before he decided to call it a day and sit down at a favorite open-air food stand to enjoy a bowl of tasty noodles or won ton and rest his feet. Arranging his finds on the table as he slowly sipped his tea, he might have the benefit of another patron's appraisal of his purchases before pocketing them and heading for home. What an agreeable way it was to spend an afternoon!

Many Westerners, however, are quickly disenchanted with archaic jade. A collector friend, after viewing an outstanding display, confided to us that none of the specimens was very attractive. She was right, if what she was looking for was the gem quality, color, and masterful carving technique of modern jade. An archaic piece no longer has a shining and polished surface. If it has been buried in a tomb, it often shows signs of calcification, which the Chinese call "rot." Chemicals in the soil, as we have already mentioned, may change its color into an undesirable hue. If the jade has been through fire, it

31. Jade trees in cloisonné pots. The flower petals are of white jade, carnelian, and amethyst; the leaf buds, turquoise.

loses its color and becomes grayish white, a type the Chinese call chicken-bone jade, which is not difficult to make.

Recently, a dealer proudly showed us six chicken-bone jade cicadas he had bought for a large sum of money. Close examination showed all six were of the same size and carved in the same pattern. Since the Han dynasty (206 B.C.–A.D. 220), the Chinese have used jade cicadas in burials. Because the stones were carved by different workers, in different ages, and at different places, they are of different sizes, shapes, and patterns. Almost no two are alike. There is no chance that suddenly six of the same size, shape, and pattern would show up as a team! Apparently some carver, quite likely a Westerner, had copied the pattern, turned out a number of them of poor-quality nephrite, and then applied the blowtorch to them.

For collectors who appreciate only the color of the stone and the intricate workmanship, it is far more rewarding to collect jade carved in modern times. During the eighteenth century, the techniques of jade-carving attained new heights as a result of the patronage of art-loving rulers like the Emperor Ch'ien-lung (1736–1795). The palace had its own atelier, and it was not unusual for a master carver to spend a good part of his life on a single piece. An unbelievable amount of time, effort, and patience goes into jade carving, which, strictly speaking, is a slow grinding process using quartz sand, carborundum dust, and other materials. A good example is the jade pagoda (*see* illustration 27) donated to the Oakland (California) Museum by the family of the late jade connoisseur, Dr. Chang Wen Ti, who personally chose and bought the jade boulder, planned and designed the project, and supervised the work. It took one hundred fifty skilled carvers ten years to finish the masterpiece.

The most magnificent jade, however, is in the Palace Museum on Taiwan. It is a jade cabbage with long white stalks and green leaves. On top of the delicate and translucent green leaves perches a pair of grasshoppers, with strongly contrasting reddish brown and dark green bodies and wings. The most beautiful parts are the legs of the insects. They show well-defined sections of red, brown, and green, rivaling those of the real grasshopper. The piece is a symphony of colors with well-orchestrated gradations of points and counterpoints. Nature produced this rare jade, and the genius of man, combining intelligence and ingenuity, cooperated to turn out the "divine piece."

During the Ch'ing dynasty (1644–1911), the palaces in Peking contained many "divine pieces," as the emperors liked to call their art treasures. At the time of the Boxer Uprising (1900), Western troops came to Peking to protect the missionaries and diplomatic personnel, and in the process did some freeloading of treasures. An old man, a family friend who had seen better days at the court, told us many years ago that he had known of a priceless piece of jade carved like half a watermelon and nearly life size. The skin was dark green; the "cut" side was red with large black spots that looked like seeds. No one could tell at a distance whether it was a real piece of watermelon or not. The jade watermelon, along with many other treasures, was lost during the sacking. The Chinese believe that a precious jade like this has a spirit and intelligence of its own. Who knows but some day it will find its way back to the world of jade lovers. After all, there is the precedent of the lost palace jade cistern rescued by the Emperor Ch'ien-lung from a monastery, where it had been used as a pickle barrel for more than four hundred years.

The term "imperial jade," for jade that once belonged to the royal family or the palace, is another fanciful term of Western creation. No doubt many of the palace jades are now in the Western countries, both in public museums and in the hands of private collectors. The large specimens can be authenticated because most of them were produced during the long reign of the Emperor Ch'ien-lung and bore engraved inscriptions in his handwriting. His calligraphy, which is supple and competent, and his poetic composition, which is mediocre, can be easily identified. However, it is quite a different thing to authenticate a piece of jewel jade as once belonging to, for instance, the infamous Dowager Empress. In the last year or two we have been shown three pieces claimed to have been owned by the wicked and beautiful monarch. The stones range from excellent to above average. The owners all paid exorbitant prices for them, no doubt more for "imperial" than for "jade."

Recently, a large quantity of jade believed to be of the nephrite variety was discovered in Taiwan (Formosa). The finished pieces show an overall green. One undesirable feature of this stone is that there are too many black graphitelike inclusions in it. In a scratch test a *dotted* white line shows, an indication of the great number of small soft particles it contains. This jade will not polish well. We have seen figurines carved out of it, and they are generously waxed to cover up the undercutting. We remember very well when this jade made its debut on the market: A fleet-footed wholesaler ordered a great number of inch-long, fan-tailed jade fish from Taiwan at a cost of perhaps $5 each. He sold these to dealers for $50 each. This was just before the opening of a big West Coast antique show. Imagine the bewilderment of the dealers when each produced his secret weapon, the jade fish, designed to stop the show and take showgoers' and fellow exhibitors' breath away.

Taiwan jade is very reasonably priced. A cabochon-cut jade of average size and uniform green color for a ring sells for about three dollars; a Burma jade of the same size and color would be worth around $50.

Other stones and gem material, such as rose quartz, smoky quartz, rock crystal, coral, amethyst, amber, carnelian, agate, and lapis lazuli, are often carved into vases, figurines, fruits, beads, and other ornamental items. They cannot be compared with jade in value, though they are quite expensive if the workmanship is good. However, glass was often used as a substitute for these semiprecious stones, but fortunately the difference is easy to detect because the glass almost always contains air bubbles. Amber can easily be synthesized—sometimes reconstituted from real amber particles and dust—and it is almost impossible to tell the difference. An amateur jeweler we know can make amber that will fool the expert. He delights in designing amber jewelry for friends. "I'll be glad to make a bracelet for your wife's birthday. Just tell me the color—butter or cherry? Clear or slightly

32. Trinket jade.

33. Large teakwood box decorated with carved serpentine. Such pieces are sometimes removed from the boxes and sold as jade. A scratch test will tell the difference.

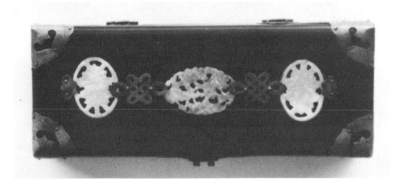

cloudy?" And then, grinning broadly, "By the way, how many bugs do you want? One bug? Two? Three?" Amber, which is fossilized resin, often contains small prehistoric insects that are preserved intact in it. Our jeweler friend obligingly swats a few gnats in his backyard and incorporates them in his creation. It should not be necessary to stress that the best procedure for the collector is to ask an expert, or to stay away from amber altogether.

All conceivable kinds of material have been used as substitutes for jade. Glass and porcelain of the celadon variety are conscious attempts to simulate jade, not with intention to cheat, but to give the items a jade look. It always pays to watch out also for natural stones used as substitutes—for instance, the white, translucent carved serpentine

34. Large carved soapstone piece of reddish color with dark reddish brown spots.

35. Soapstone bookends, greenish white color, have carved and pierced designs on both the front and back.

36. Soapstone figurine of a fisherman.

37. Soapstone statuette of Kwan-yin, goddess of compassion.

pieces often found decorating Chinese wooden, lacquer, or brass boxes. When these come off the boxes, they are sometimes intentionally—but more often unintentionally—sold as mutton-fat jade (white jade of the highest quality, so called because it looks like congealed mutton fat). Grape clusters and other greenish fruits carved from natural stone are often not jade; they cannot stand an honest-to-goodness scratch test, since they are made from such substitutes as bowenite, serpentine, and soapstone.

Finally, a word about soapstone. We were shocked to see, at an antique show, a pair of soapstone bookends carved with a floral design that bore a price tag of $50. In China on festival days, before World War II, bookends of this sort were sold at sidewalk stands for about 10 or 20 cents a pair. Often they would be damaged or broken before the buyer got them home because soapstone is notoriously soft —you can scratch it with your fingernail or even bite off a piece. Of course, a toiling, inglorious carver with real talent sometimes created items of artistic value out of soapstone. Such specimens would be worthwhile in spite of the cheap material from which they are made.

If you have been hankering for a jade, just one piece to fondle or to carry with you at all times, in the belief that it indeed has a healing quality to soothe your spirit when you are tired, to cheer you when you are dejected, and if one day you see such a jade piece, be it archaic or modern, and immediately fall in love with it, it is your jade. Go in and buy it. It will be worth all the money you spend on it.

38. Carved soapstone inlaid in wood.

39. Carved soapstone inlaid in wood.

THE GRAPHIC ARTS
PAINTING AND CALLIGRAPHY

IN CHINA DOWN THROUGH THE AGES, SCHOLARS AND ANTIQUARIANS collected calligraphy, painting, archaic bronze, jade, and ceramics—in that order. Pottery tomb animals and human figures of the Han and T'ang periods were not sought after, on account of their association with the dead, a relationship the Chinese do not like. In the case of archaic bronze and jade that also came from the tombs, this association was conveniently overlooked—the Chinese have always had a marked ability to rationalize.

Once the door to China was opened, however, Western connoisseurs constantly searched for tomb figures, with the result that many clever potters around Peking began to devote their full time to the making of "T'ang horses." On the other hand, Western collectors have always had difficulty in appreciating the twin products of the versatile Chinese brush—painting and calligraphy, though many will vigorously deny such a statement.

We have often been shown paintings by the Ming dynasty artist Shên Chou or by the great Japanese artist Sesshū, bought either in Peking or in Kyoto from "reliable dealers" or private collectors. These can indeed look very much like authentic works, for the copyists were often clever and talented artists who had turned cynical and mercenary through frustration. Landscapes by the literati school were easy to copy. Another favorite for the copyists was the Italian Jesuit priest

Giuseppe Castiglione (Lang Shih-ning). He served the emperors K'ang-hsi, Yung-chêng, and Ch'ien-lung, who liked to have around them a foreigner who could paint in the Chinese way; and he was popular in the West because he was another Marco Polo, but one who could also paint. At a recent antique show, a forged Castiglione was actually priced at $18,000.

Castiglione became an easy victim of the copyist, because he did not have early and intensive training in the use of the Chinese brush, which was the all-important tool. There were rare cases of painters who chose to paint with the fingers or even with the tongue, but essentially it is the brush that gives the painting the important quality of vitality, rhythm, and life.

The brush was supposedly invented around 200 B.C., though recent evidence puts it at a much earlier time. Paper first appeared in China around A.D. 100. Before the invention of the brush and paper, writing was done by carving on bamboo strips with a knife or stylus. Even after the invention of paper, writing continued to be done with the brush on bamboo strips because paper was expensive.

It is perhaps profitable here to examine the brush. Soft brushes are made from goat hair; stiff ones require the hair of the rabbit and wolf. Since brushes also come in many sizes, the artist has at his disposal a wide choice varying in both dimensions and degree of stiffness. Sometimes several brushes are fastened together in a row for the flat wash of a large area.

The ink must be freshly ground by rubbing an ink stick on an inkstone. Then the brush is allowed to soak up the proper amount of ink to spread on the paper for a specific purpose—for instance, the painting of flower petals and leaves. On the other hand, a dry brush is called for in drawing the rocks and gnarled trunks of pine trees common in oriental paintings. In watching the artist work, one sees him constantly working his brush on the inkstone to get the right amount of ink to achieve the desired spread and shade. If color is used, he proceeds in the same way. Such is the nature of the highly absorbent Chinese paper that each brushstroke must be thought out in advance and then applied with swiftness and assurance, since no correction is possible.

▶

40. *Eight Horses* by Lang Shih-ning, Ch'ing dynasty. Lang Shih-ning is the Chinese name taken by Giuseppe Castiglione, the Italian priest who became a favorite of Emperor Ch'ien-lung. *Collection of the National Palace Museum, Taipei, Taiwan, Republic of China*

42. Reproduction of stone rubbing showing calligraphy of fine structural quality.

To be proficient in brushwork, a man serves a long apprenticeship of intensive training in calligraphy, which is considered the mark, and perhaps the most important mark, of a good education. As recently as, say, thirty years ago, a person's education and even his character were judged by his calligraphy. A job-seeker had to present a page of his calligraphy to a prospective employer before he was hired. This was considered as necessary as an interview in the West.

At the age of six or seven, the child of an educated family would spend one or two hours each day on calligraphic lessons. Stone-rubbing reproductions of T'ang and Sung calligraphies, noted for their fine structural qualities, served as his first models. At the age of ten or twelve, he moved on to the Wei dynasty stele rubbings noted for austere stylistic elegance and semiarchaic flavor. At fifteen or sixteen, he progressed to copying the earliest form of Chinese writing, rubbings from stone drums and archaic bronzes. This intensive training was designed to make him not only understand and appreciate the beauty of all

◄

41. Imitation of Castiglione's horses, including his Chinese signature. Note the lack of shading and poor perspective; also the difference in the conformation of the horses.

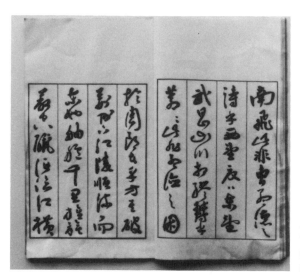

43. The highly expressive "running" or "grass" styles, reproduced from old calligraphy books.

the types of scripts used in the three thousand years of Chinese writing, but absorb the spirit of the styles as well because, in graphic arts, the Chinese believe that copying is the best means of training for an artist. In the meantime, he would also practice with a heavy "steel brush," a pointed steel rod the size of a large brush, on a sand pan without any support under his arm, to develop steadiness of arm and wrist. Only after all this rigorous and exhaustive training would he be allowed to develop his own style. The arduous and time-consuming process must be endured before he was considered prepared to take up the twin arts of calligraphy and painting.

Chinese calligraphy offers the same aesthetic satisfaction as painting. Chinese characters developed from pictures. Calligraphy is therefore painting in abstract. Perhaps it is as abstract as music. Certainly viewing calligraphy has the same hypnotic fascination as following the flight of a conductor's baton in its rhythmical sweeps and cadences and the sudden surge of power in its overall smooth and graceful movements. Both calligraphy and painting share, to a large extent, this quality—restless and yet rhythmic movement, and the ever-present spirit or life force behind it. In an oriental painting the wind always blows in the willows, the water ripples, the dragon moves in and out of clouds, the curtains and the trains of garments flutter, the hand points instead of lying indolently on the arm of the chair. Even in the quietest landscape, the mountain ranges march, the rocks beetle. The spirit or life force is always moving or ready to move. This is the result of brush-work, swiftly and assuredly executed. Oriental painting may lack chiaroscuro, perspective, but it has aesthetic qualities Western art cannot impart to the viewer. Viewing oriental paintings offers a different but equally satisfying experience.

The earliest paintings were figures and portraits of historical personages for didactic or edifying purposes. None of them are now in existence. The recently discovered tomb painting of an aristocratic lady dating from the Chou dynasty is perhaps the earliest example. Others such as "Gentlemen Watching a Fight," a tomb painting now in the Boston Museum of Fine Arts, and the genre painting done in lacquer on a basket, discovered in a tomb in the Chinese colony of Lolang in North Korea, are all of the Han dynasty. They reveal the powerful calligraphic lines that were to become the dominant feature of Chinese art. Figure painting continued to be the main form from the end of Han to the beginning of the T'ang dynasty. A few existing examples attributed to the various artists of this period are extant, such as Ku K'ai-chih's "Admonition of an Imperial Instructress." Even though they may not be authentic works, they are at least faithful copies. They show that Chinese figure painting had attained maturity.

During the early period, Chinese artists were in a sense merely artisans, or decorators and illustrators, serving the wishes of the court, doing murals and frescoes at the command of the rulers. The less fortunate ones eked out their living working for the increasingly popular religion of Buddhism. They seldom painted to express their own feelings, nor did they sign their works.

Landscape painting was still in its infancy, landscapes merely serving as background for the subject matter then popular. During the T'ang dynasty, perhaps the most creative period in Chinese history, it was emerging as an independent branch that would overshadow, in later ages, all the other categories. In the beginning, landscapes were formal and stylized. These tours de force, in predominantly blue and green or green and gold, with jagged peaks "high rising" into the clouds where, according to popular belief, the Taoist goddess queen held her court, were favored by the rulers, many of whom were ardent Taoist believers.

However, a revolt was in the making, and Chinese landscape painting was to divide into the Northern school and the Southern school.*

---

* Chinese writers made much of the distinction between the two schools. However, their differences, particularly during the later ages, are so elusive and confusing that Westerners can very well ignore them.

The finest and truly monumental works were produced immediately before and during the early Sung dynasty (907–1126.) During the late Sung period, the elements of austere and remote grandeur were slowly humanized and softened by viewing nature through its many moods. This poetic treatment became increasingly popular.

The Sung emperors, although woefully inadequate as administrators and empire builders, were notable for their encouragement of and active part in the arts. Some of them indeed could stand on their own as painters and calligraphers. The range of subjects expanded until it became all-inclusive. Nothing was too small or too insignificant for the artist: animals, birds, flowers, insects, and fish. Bamboo became a specialized subject. It was the area where calligraphic virtuosity could be best exploited.

By means of imperial examinations, painters were chosen to be artists in residence at the imperial academy; these painters were often referred to as academicians. But this was an age of such versatility and cultural excellence that most of the men who served as high officials were poets and literary men who also dabbled in painting, and they became known as literary painters. Away from the court, there were many talented artists who chose to avoid the narrow critical standards set by the emperor and his circle and to be guided only by their own conscience and beliefs. These painters, notably the Ch'an Buddhists (in Japan, the Zen sect) and the Taoist philosophers, formed an important tributary of the mainstream of Chinese art. We shall meet them again later on.

Many delightful stories are told of the examinations that selected artists for the imperial academy. At least one bears repeating here because it throws light on the artistic trend of the time (circa 1000 to 1300): The subject matter at one examination was a line of poetry, "The fragrance of crushed petals follows the hoofs of the returning horse." It was considered impossible to depict the scent of fallen petals under a horse's hoofs, but one artist achieved the impossible and took top honors. He painted a scholar riding home alone between mountains full of flowering trees. On this lonely trail, where the man and his horse seemed to be the only living things, two butterflies hovered closely behind the horse's hoofs.

The unfortunate consequence was that academicians increasingly sought to achieve fame by following the methods popular and fashionable at the court, and scholars and literary men who dabbled in painting resorted to what was derogatorily known as "ink-play" at the end of the Sung dynasty. However, this type of literary men's painting achieved great popularity during the later Ming and Ch'ing periods. In landscapes, which were becoming more and more evocative and even sentimental, human beings became insignificant accessories, discernible only in hermit-scholars' garments or serving the necessary role in pastoral scenes where the homing fishing boat would be lost without the guidance of human intelligence.

The emergence of landscapes as the major form of graphic art spearheaded the trend of Chinese painting up to the present century. The great heritage of portrait and figure painting became less and less honored, though technically it is more demanding to paint portraits and human figures. A portrait artist must spend his lifetime in exclusive devotion to his art. Not so the landscape artist. With minimum practice, poets and literary men, who were necessarily accomplished calligraphers, could easily transfer their talent to landscape painting as another form of self-expression. With the emergence of the literati school, another convention was firmly established—namely, the marriage of painting, poetry, and calligraphy. After completing a picture, the artist would ask all his friends—painters, and literary men, and poets like himself—to compose poems and write in the ample space provided at the top of the picture for that purpose. No doubt this custom served to stimulate interest and congeniality. But, at its worst, it resembled the self-serving efforts of a mutual admiration society, though for the collectors of later ages, the practice has proved a valuable aid in authentication.

Chinese painting had, by the end of the Sung dynasty, attained maturity in all its traditional divisions: human figures and things; landscapes; palaces and buildings; animals, flowers, and birds; grass and insects; and bamboo. The imperial collections of old and contemporary works were so rich that, had they survived, our knowledge of that era as well as of those preceding it would have been greatly increased.

When the Mongols swept away the weakened Southern Sung and established the short-lived Yüan dynasty, most artists refused to serve the barbarous conquerors and chose to live in voluntary exile and retirement. We have mentioned the Ch'an painters who ignored the court-oriented rules and standards and delivered their esoteric message by powerful abbreviated strokes. Now they were joined by the literary painters themselves. It was a period of reassessment for these artists. Their unhurried approach in composition and their conscientiousness in searching for technical refinement were greatly admired by later ages. The greatest masters of the Yüan dynasty were to exert much influence during the following centuries.

The Ming dynasty that succeeded the short Mongolian rule offered hope of a renaissance of the arts. It was unthinkable for the Ming

44. Figure painting of Taoist immortals by Ch'en Tsao-hua, Ch'ing dynasty.

ruling house to model itself on the politically disastrous Sung dynasty; therefore it sought to emulate many of the ideals of the great T'ang period. But overemphasis on Confucian philosophy and court intrigues soon destroyed this forward outlook. The late Ming period became markedly self-complacent and withdrawn. In painting, the literati school maintained supremacy and talented artists were produced. There were also attempts by artists themselves to solidify techniques, to establish canons, and to form schools, often named after geographical locations. These meaningless divisions have no place in our short résumé.

The unrest at the end of this dynasty invited the takeover by the Manchus, who founded the Ch'ing dynasty. Although the Manchu emperors became addicted to Chinese culture at an early stage of their rule, among artists there was again a large number of nonconformists and eccentrics—notably, as before, the Ch'an monks and Taoist philosophers. Perhaps the best example is Chu Ta, or Pa-ta-shan-jên. Being related to the ruling house of the Ming dynasty, he had to become a monk to avoid persecution. Chu Ta looked at the world with a jaundiced eye, and his subjects were often whimsical and humorous. He painted swiftly, using strong, economical strokes. (The contemporary painter Ch'i Pai-shih is quite like him in his choice of subject matter and in his brushstrokes.) He would not paint for money. To paint he had to be in the mood; and this usually happened after he had been wined and dined. Once, however, not quite in the mood and annoyed by his host's insistence, he picked up the brush and drew a nondescript shape like a tray. Then he threw away the brush, lifted the inkstone, and hurled it on the paper. After Chu himself had sailed out of the door, the chagrined host took a look at the mess. And there it was—a perfect picture of an eagle perched on a big rock and ready to fly! No brush could have created such a "divine piece."

Another eccentric painter refused the repeated calls of a court official. To avoid punishment, he pretended to be insane. Finally the official held the artist's father as hostage and sent the painter word that unless he came and painted a picture for him, his father would never be set free. The "insane" painter appeared, filthy and in tatters. He asked for a tub of freshly ground ink and a large piece of paper, which he spread on the ground. Then he shed his tatters until he stood completely naked before the official (intentionally insulting behavior, of course). Next he submerged himself in the tub of ink, did one quick somersault on the paper, and was gone. On the paper the spreading ink took the shape of a life-sized lion. The imprint of the artist's hands and feet became the animal's four paws; the imprint of his body became the lion's body, and his unkempt long hair produced the lion's shaggy mane. It was again a "divine piece"! Such popular legends, true or not, illustrate the admiration given the independent spirit of the true artist and his revolt against convention—here, even his revolt against the sacred brush itself, and therefore the ultimate revolt.

In Japan, the early graphic arts showed strong Chinese influence, although there was a difference between the Chinese school (Kara-e) and the Japanese school (Yamato-e), which was noted for its decorative use of colors and its approach to landscape painting, using the gentler native scenery as inspiration.* Another distinction, also follow-

---

* Specifically, we should mention the Tosa school, whose heritage is best exemplified by the long horizontal hand scrolls with lively and often humorous genre scenes; and the Kanō school, which, according to such an early authority as Professor Ernest Fenollosa, is not only a faithful follower of the Chinese tradition, but the sole custodian of the great Sung tradition! These two schools both exerted their influence on the decorative art of the Edo period and even on the plebeian wood-block prints.

45. Openly acknowledging her debt to the great flower painter Yün Shou-p'ing, Miss Ch'en Wei (probably nineteenth century) did a good job imitating the great master of the Ch'ing dynasty.

46. Japanese screen in polychrome color, a fine example of the art of the Kanō School. Late seventeenth century. *Stanford University Museum*

ing the Chinese tradition, was that between the professional and the literary painters (Bun-jin-ga). Some of the most prominent Japanese artists visited China, and studied and collected the great masters of the Sung dynasty. Their works were highly praised by their Chinese contemporaries. However, the brushwork of the Japanese artists often betrayed self-consciousness and a tendency toward exaggerated strokes. For the professional painters, patronage was not lacking from the opulent ruling class whose taste ran to immense screens and sliding doors in lavish gold and gay colors, which served to brighten the dark interiors of their mansions and castles.

It was the Japanese who first achieved artistic communication with the West. "Pictures of the floating world" (ukiyo-e)—or wood-block prints as they were known outside Japan—were originally intended to be mass-produced art for the middle-class merchants, who could not afford giant screens and did not have the place to accommodate them. These prints became immensely popular, and many talented artists devoted their efforts to this new medium. Instead of producing the imitative and anemic landscapes approved by the tea-masters, these men created numerous pictures that satisfied the healthy and robust middle-class taste for action, drama, humor, pathos, and even fashion. The realism pervading these pictures was further accentuated by the strong, heavy lines of this particular medium. Said a critic of Hiroshege (1797–1858), "His rain is wet indeed." His raindrops appear like hailstones pelting down with all the violence of nature on the ephemeral world.

In Korea, accomplishments in the realm of graphic art had already reached an impressive stage during the period from the fourth to the sixth century, as demonstrated by the recently discovered tomb murals. Unfortunately, paintings of later ages, like many other Korean art treasures, were thoroughly and mercilessly destroyed by repeated foreign invasions. But during the more recent long-reigning Yi dynasty many paintings were preserved, and they testify to the fact that Korean artists equaled and sometimes surpassed the best in China and Japan during the same period.

Readers may wonder why we have not discussed specific artists individually. Art and artists are indeed inseparable, but works of ancient masters like Wu Tao-tzū are no longer in existence. Only a small number of Sung paintings are extant, and it is debatable how many of them are authentic. (The Chinese say that nine out of ten of the Sung paintings are copies.) Many writers therefore fall back on

47. Wood-block print in color
by Kunisada (1786–1864).

48. Original painting for a
wood-block print on semi-
transparent paper. The artist
made a change in the center
of the picture by adding a
stone lantern, which he
pasted in.

the practice of hashing and rehashing old Chinese commentaries, which are at best vague and ambiguous. Talking about the "verve," the "immediacy," and the "boldness" of the "monumental work of Wu-tao-tzū" and of others whose paintings are no longer in existence seems to us an exercise in futility. We believe the reader will find our brief general survey of Chinese painting more useful and informative. After all, most oriental masters of the Ming and Ch'ing periods are already in museums, and the small number in private hands cannot be acquired without paying a fortune. Therefore we feel that collectors who appreciate oriental art should try to make their own discoveries. A quotation from Chinese poetry seems appropriate:

Every generation, among the rivers and mountains new talents appear,
Each will lead the trend of art for the next five hundred years.

Many admirable artists are now working in the Far East and in Western countries, and we believe it is both more interesting and more worthwhile to collect the works of a struggling artist who impresses you. Perhaps ten or fifteen years later you will find that the world too has discovered him. A few years ago, a collection of Ch'i Pai-shih (1861–1957) was exhibited at a major West Coast museum. It was loaned by a retired Japanese diplomat who had served in China before World War II. Impressed by Ch'i's paintings, he got to know the artist and began collecting his works. Now he owns the largest and the best collection of Ch'i's work.

Ch'i started life as a carpenter. But nature fascinated him. During his leisure time, he would collect insects, crabs, and shrimp and enjoy watching them. Next he tried to paint them. Finally he traded his hammer and saw for the brush. No academician, Ch'i used powerful and economical brushstrokes—what the Chinese call "the big sword and broad ax" technique, a quality greatly admired by Chinese connoisseurs.

Ch'i is universally recognized as one of the greatest oriental artists, if not the greatest, of the twentieth century. He lived to be ninety-six years old and was still productive at that age, painting several pictures a day. His paintings are still available, but there are many imitations on the market.

Two years ago at an estate sale, we acquired two paintings by Chang Shu-chi (1900–1957) for a song. When this writer was a student at the National Central University, Chang was head of the Department of Chinese Painting. During World War II, he was commissioned to paint a scroll of one hundred doves to be presented to

49. Shrimp by Ch'i Pai-shih. Ink on paper. The artist is noted for his powerful but sensitive calligraphic brushstrokes.

50. Chicks by Ch'i Pai-shih. Ink and slight color.

51. Rats stealing eggs under a sputtering candle by Ch'i Pai-shih. The couplet says, "The candlelight is as bright as the noonday. How can we be accused of stealing if we are not afraid of being seen?" A competent defense, perhaps.

the White House as a token of appreciation for American help. He visited this country, and later took up residence in Berkeley, California. We went to see him several times before his untimely death in 1957. Chang's flowers and birds, done in exquisite colors, are alive with a subtle and luminous quality. He did many pictures during his sojourn in California. Most of his works now on the market are reproductions, but once in a while one comes upon an original piece.

52. Butterflies and lilies. Watercolor by Chang Shu-chi.

In the same university where Chang taught, Hsü Pei-hung (1893–1953), who headed the Department of Western Painting, also painted in Chinese style. His favorite subject was horses. Hsü was internationally well known, and many of his works are in the United States. Another professor, Chang Ta-ch'ien, has been living in the Western Hemisphere since World War II, and has studios in the United States. Works of these two versatile artists can be found on the market.

There are younger oriental artists too. Many of them are personal friends with whom this writer shared a memorable wartime experience on the beautiful university campus overlooking the Chialing River in Chungking. It would be unfair to list some and not the others. For a list of contemporary Chinese painters, we recommend Michael Sullivan's book, *Chinese Art in the Twentieth Century,* University of California Press. The names are listed both in Chinese and in English and accompanied by short biographical notes.

The following categories, though collectible, do not belong in the realm of art:

1. *Ancestral portraits:* Many of these were done by commercial artists with the aid of snapshots of the deceased. Before the invention of photography, such an artist kept in his studio portraits with various standard facial features, and the client had to select the one most like his forebear. Then the artist, using the chosen face as a guide, would paint a portrait resembling it, dressing the person in mandarin costume. A considerable number of these portraits now grace American living rooms. It must be mentioned, though, that countless others were made for export to satisfy the demand for orientalia, and in no sense represented anybody's ancestors.

2. *Paintings on mirrors and glass: See* Chapter 8.

3. *Paintings on the so-called "rice paper":* These were done by

53. Magpies on a persimmon tree, by Chang I-chou.

54. Landscape by Ma Chi-ou. With good training in brushwork and inspiration from the great Sung artists, this young painter (during the late 1940s) turned out very creditable work.

56. The quick but sure brushwork imparts a sense of movement to the galloping horse by Paul Fu, who now lives in the United States.

55. Landscape by Ma Chi-ou, late 1940s.

57. Painting on a fan of children making a snowman, by Ch'en Ta-chang. Ink and slight color. Ca. 1940.

58. Chinese family scene, watercolor on silk. Though it belongs to the category of commercial art, it is certainly a competent, detailed work of the early nineteenth century.

聖誕

59. A Chinese commercial artist's interpretation of the Nativity, watercolor on silk. Ca. 1900.

hacks on a type of material called "Tung Tsao," made from the pith of grass and also used in herb medicine. It is porous and can be pressed down to dry. When the wet brush touches the surface, the part that gets the ink rises and creates a relief effect. The subject matter is often scenes of opium dens and oriental tortures. These paintings degrade the painter as well as the collector.

4. *Religious paintings:* Scrolls and banners using Buddhist or Taoist themes and made for religious services are collectible. Quite a number of them, poorly done on cheap material, were made for the export or tourist trade. Occasionally Christian subjects were used.

60. Opium den scene painted on the so-called rice paper.

61. Buddhist painting, originally a banner or hanging of the Tibetan sect. Tempera-type color on fabric.

6

COLLECTING ORIENTAL CERAMICS

A SMALL PEACH BLOOM VASE WAS SOLD IN NEW YORK FOR $18,000 in 1886. It created such a sensation all over the United States at the time that numerous copies were made in glass, and now the glass imitations are selling for over $150. However, these prices pale in the light of what happened recently. A Ming porcelain jar that had been used as an umbrella stand in an English home brought over half a million dollars!

Occasionally the newspapers carry the story of a dusty old vase (found in some attic or basement) that turned out to be a rare piece appraised at $35,000. Accounts like this, combined with the terrific rise in the prices paid for antique oriental ceramics, make one wonder how great the chances are of striking it rich in this field. In short, can the ordinary collector stumble on such valuable treasure by browsing in secondhand stores or small antique shops? Can you?

Yes, you can—though the chances are rare, *very* rare.

Here is what is more likely to happen: You wander into an antique shop hoping this is your lucky day. In a locked showcase there is a ceramic piece that looks unusual to you, and you ask the dealer to see it.

Instead, he reaches under the counter and comes up with a thick book called *Complete Antique Prices,* or something like that, and quickly opens it to a place already marked by a slip of paper.

"See here. 'Chinese Chün ware jar (circa 1000), 4¼ inches tall, price approximately $42,000.' "

Then he takes the ceramic piece carefully from the case. "Here it is. Compare it with the picture yourself." You strain to see the details in the fuzzy ¼ by ½-inch picture.

"Same? Okay! Let me show you something else." He takes out a tape measure. "Exactly 4¼ inches, see? Too bad the picture isn't in color. I'm sure the color is exactly the same."

If you are endowed with a high degree of suspicion (which, by the way, is not a bad quality for a collector to have), you might question whether the tenth-century Chinese mass-produced their jars exactly 4¼ inches in height. And if, by chance, you have just returned from a vacation in Mexico, you may be disturbed by an area where the body of the jar shows through the glaze and reminds you strongly of the red porous Mexican wares. (Always examine the clay or body wherever it shows.)

You are right to be disturbed. The jar is a copy made in Mexico, but copies of oriental porcelains have been made all over the world. When you turn this jar over and examine the foot area (and you should do this), you can even see the number 867. The tenth-century Chinese did not use Arabic numerals! The dealer, however, is interested only in evidence substantiating his claim. He will stubbornly refuse to see anything to discredit it. So don't risk turning the jar over again to prove your point. Facing you is the ubiquitous sign: "Beautiful to look at—but if you break it, you have bought it." Anything can happen in an argument—even a gentlemanly one—and you don't want to pay $42,000 for something worth less than 42 cents.

We hasten to add that the dealer may not be knowingly dishonest. Everybody nowadays is overaware of hidden treasures, and he may just have developed big ideas; quite a few do.

Oriental ceramics is a complicated and difficult subject. Much is known about it, thanks to the intensive research done by Western and oriental scholars during the last hundred years, but a great deal still remains unknown or uncertain. Every bit of new knowledge and new evidence will help fit a few more of the missing pieces into the gigantic puzzle.

To the serious collector, three things are absolutely necessary as a means of increasing his knowledge: reading on the subject, seeing as many specimens as possible, and feeling them with his own hands.

There is no lack of reading and research material, but space limitations prevent our listing more than a few "musts." First there is the compendium by Warren E. Cox, *The Book of Pottery and Porcelain,* which runs to more than 1,100 pages and contains about 1,500 pictures.

It is good for reference and is also interesting to read. Another must is *Chinese Pottery and Porcelain* by R. L. Hobson, with whom Cox often disagrees—sometimes violently. Last but not least is *The Ceramic Art of China and Other Countries of the Far East,* by W. B. Honey. There are many others, and mountains of material have appeared in periodicals and special publications. It is worthwhile for the advanced collector to examine all these sources and glean as much information as he can from them. But, for the beginner, at least the aforementioned books should be kept at hand for reference.

The next important step—seeing all the available specimens—means going to museums. Pictures, even those in the most expensive art books, are not dependable; nothing is quite as informative as seeing the real things. A good museum collection has pieces representing the different periods, and through repeated visits the collector will develop his ability to recognize body, shape, form, and style, as well as to differentiate amongst the glazes and enamels of the various periods. For instance, a carmine or rose enamel used in famille rose will never appear on a Ming piece. And most porcelains decorated in underglaze blue cannot be attributed to a period earlier than the thirteenth century. Eventually, from just an overall impression of a piece, the collector will be skilled enough to say that it has the Ming look, or the K'ang-hsi style. He may even disagree sometimes with the attribution the museum has given to a certain specimen. This is perfectly all right. Museums are not infallible and their dating is not always final. As new evidence comes to light, they sometimes must amend their dating. Any museum with specimens 95 percent authentic and attributions 85 percent correct is way above average. The staff of the Palace Museum on Taiwan often tells visitors: "We are absolutely sure of our porcelains." Their certainty is based on the fact that the pieces have been in the collection for many centuries, some from the time they were made. Examined and authenticated by generations of experts, they perhaps include no fakes. But today scholars are challenging the attributions of even such an astute collector as the Emperor Ch'ien-lung himself!

Personally handling authentic pieces is, of course, easier recommended than achieved. Museums certainly do not permit it. But if the beginner is fortunate enough to know anyone with a large private collection, he should seek permission to handle as many authentic specimens as possible.

He should examine, with a magnifying glass, the paste, the glaze, and even the bubbles in the glaze, and carefully note the differences between the objects of the various periods. Next, he should run his fingers over the surface, particularly the area around the foot. He will keep in mind, of course, that not until the Ch'ing dynasty were vases made with grooves on the foot to accommodate the wooden stands that had become fashionable and almost indispensable. Through book study he should already have learned that the Ming foot tends to be massive and heavy; that the early Yüeh ware has spur marks very similar to some of the Korean celadons, a resemblance by which scholars were able to prove the early Yüeh influence on the latter; that some wares are glazed inside the foot but not on the foot; that others are glazed on the foot too; and some were fired on spurs and others on sand piles. Also, that the Ting ware of the Sung dynasty and some Ying Ch'ing (shadow blue), particularly the thin and delicate type, were fired upside down because otherwise they would have collapsed. (As a result they had rough lips,* and to cover these up, copper or silver rings were often fitted over the unglazed lips.)

However, not until the collector can turn the different samples of different periods over and around, compare them, scrutinize them under a magnifying glass, close his eyes and feel them with his hands—not until then can he understand the subtle differences and be truly prepared to appreciate what the experts have written.

The Early Period

Pottery making is often the first necessary industry of a people entering the threshold of civilization. In the Far East, the Chinese are perhaps the earliest craftsmen in this field. The early red pottery and black pottery culture dates from 3000–2500 B.C. Geographically it covers the general area along the course of the Yellow River. In the Yangtze valley and in the extreme south, similar activities must have been going on, but less is known about them. The Shang-Chou period is noted for its bronzes, though pottery vessels were also made, including a fine whiteware, and some of them appear to have been glazed.

Ceramic production first assumed importance during the Han dynasty. Bronze vessels were expensive, and the protoporcelain that had attained stoneware hardness became a satisfactory substitute. The wares showed a great deal of similarity, both in shape and decoration, to the bronze vessels. Even the predominantly green and brown glazes suggested the color of bronze patina. A large number of the items were manufactured for burials, including miniature models of houses, stoves,

---

* Some writers believe that these fine and delicate wares with rough lips were fired right side up on some sort of ingenious contrivance.

62. Prehistoric Chinese red pottery jar, ca. 3000–2000 B.C. *Stanford University Museum*

and utensils; figurines representing attendants, servants, guards, and domestic animals. The green lead glaze on these objects, after long burial, acquires a beautiful iridescence and is hard to fake.

The Han was an expansionist empire that adopted the policy of offense as the best defense toward the warlike nomadic tribes in the north and northwest, in order to keep the trade routes open. This led authorities to speculate that the lead glaze on Han wares was introduced from foreign countries, although the Chinese had used glaze nearly a thousand years before.

The next great empire, T'ang, was both expansionist and internationalist in outlook. People of all nations and faiths congregated in its affluent capital, and its cultural influence spread far and wide. Japan, for instance, sent students and borrowed extensively from the T'ang Chinese, but China also received a great deal in return. Mideastern craftsmen brought their technique of making fine metalwares, which exerted considerable influence upon the shape and form of Chinese ceramics. Greek motifs were also generously adopted. Three-color glazes were used in tones of green, olive, olive brown, yellow, and reddish orange. Occasionally a blue was used, perhaps derived from cobalt. The glazes were kept within bounds by incised and pressed relief patterns. The potting showed great strength, freedom, and vitality. The tomb figurines and animals became a genuine sculptural art. It was these items that later drew the greatest interest of Western collectors. To satisfy the demand, hundreds and thousands of copies of T'ang tomb horses and camels were made during the nineteenth and twentieth centuries; some were even rebuilt from broken pieces.

At the end of the T'ang period, a fine, thin whiteware made its appearance; it fits the Western definition of porcelain. The appearance of porcelain appropriately marks the end of the early period of Chinese ceramic history.

63. Protoporcelain jar with green lead glaze, Han dynasty. Long burial caused the glaze to develop iridescence. *Stanford University Museum*

64. Urn with three-color (yellow, brown, and green) glaze, T'ang dynasty. *Stanford University Museum*

The Middle Period

The next period, the Sung dynasty (including the short period of division immediately preceding it), was universally recognized as the classical period, and the most magnificent in Chinese ceramic history. Politically, it was a tragic series of attempts to buy peace at any price, and failing repeatedly. Culturally, however, there is much to commend this unfortunate period that produced many of the greatest Chinese paintings and, in ceramics, perhaps the world's very best, not to be excelled by later ages.

Among its ceramic productions are the Kuan ware (the imperial ware), a white or grayish glazed ware sometimes tinged with a subtle blue or green; the rare Ju ware with a blue glaze of various shades; and the Chün ware, predominantly blue but often with the so-called transmutation glaze of dramatic violet, purple, red, buff, or turquoise green. The colors resulted from the action of the minerals (iron and copper) in the glaze and in the body, and the conditions during the firing. At first the colors were entirely uncontrolled, even unexpected. The story goes that when the dramatic red and violet purple first appeared, the frightened potters fled the area, thinking they had angered the kiln god. These wares do not exactly fit the definition of porcelain and are more correctly described as stoneware because the body is light buff, whitish gray, or dark gray. But they served as a better vehicle for the thickly applied, sleek, rich, and unctuous glaze that was a result of the constant effort by the Chinese to make imitation jade. It is largely the glaze that makes the Sung wares incomparable in beauty.

There is another type of stoneware often overlooked by Chinese connoisseurs but greatly admired by Westerners: the T'zu-chou ware. This was often decorated with a creamy white or dark brown-black slip and boldly incised, carved, or painted in strongly contrasting colors, sometimes with the addition of red and green. The potting is robust and strong; the designs show sweeping calligraphic strokes and certainly can be considered as the forerunner of the painted wares of later Ming and Ch'ing periods. There was great freedom in the decoration and spontaneous humor, for the ware was made for the common people. For instance, a ceramic pillow bears an inscribed admonition for the user: "Don't talk among crowds, and go home early if you have nothing to do"—certainly wise advice to follow in a monarchial regime.

True porcelains, meaning those that meet the exacting Western standard of high-fired, white, translucent body paste, were represented by Ting ware, and Ying Ch'ing, which is very much like Ting except that it has a greenish or bluish tinge where the glaze has pooled in the

65. Headrest, Tz'u Chou ware; Sung dynasty. *Stanford University Museum*

designs. These wares, which were copied all over China, may be the forerunners of modern-day porcelain.

The above-mentioned wares—the Kuan, Chün, Ting, Ying Ch'ing, Ju—and a type of olive brown and olive green celadon richly covered with incised or pressed patterns and known as Northern celadon, or Tung ware, were made at the kilns in the north when the Sung capital was at K'ai-fêng. When the Chin Tartars captured the capital and the art-loving emperor, the Sung court fled south and established a capital at the beautiful lake-city, Hangchow. Their cultural pursuits were continued with nostalgic wistfulness. This politically inept but culturally unexcelled period was known as the Southern Sung (1127–1279). There, awaiting the refugee court, was a solid base of ceramic-making technology that had been in existence since the Han dynasty.

Yüeh ware,* a celadon, had for several hundreds of years served as the palace ware of the rulers of the local principalities. Now, Lungch'üan, the most prominent of its kind produced by kilns near Hangchow, a ware of beautiful green and bluish green, became synonymous for Chinese celadon ware. As early as the late T'ang period, Chinese celadon was exported all over Asia and the Near East. A number of

* Believed to be the ancestor of most of the celadon wares in the Far East, including the Chinese Northern celadon, the Lung-ch'üan, and the Korean (Koryŏ) celadon.

pieces of this ware were discovered over the last hundred years in the Philippines and other Pacific islands, and were much publicized so that they attracted considerable attention in the collecting world. Not surprisingly, therefore, a good many imitations made recently in the Far East are being sold today as "Sung or Yüan celadons discovered in the Philippines." Some of them are so new that you can still see the kiln gloss.

As one authority aptly put it: "The celadon is the backbone of Chinese ceramics." Except for Chün, Ting, and Ying Ch'ing (shadow blue), wares with heavy, unctuous glazes like massed lard in various shades of green, blue, gray, and brown belong largely to this category. Color depends upon a combination of factors, such as the mineral content of the clay and of the glaze and also the firing, over which the potters at that time had little control; therefore, no two early celadons are exactly alike in color.

Wares that had achieved fame during the Northern Sung period were now made in the south. Among them was Kuan ware, now known as Southern Kuan ware. It has a dark body under a pale green, blue, whitish gray, or rice color (meaning unpolished rice) glaze. The nearly black body is the result of high iron content in the clay around Hangchow. Critics often refer to this type as having a brown lip (where the glaze ran thin) and an iron foot (where the glaze stopped short of the edge).

Many potters who had made the Chün ware in the north fled south, at the time of the Tartar invasion, to Fatshan or Shekwan near Canton, and carried on their tradition. Their stoneware body and flambé glazes are often superficially indistinguishable from the original Chün. W. B. Honey mentions that of the thirty or so Chün specimens bought by the great collector George Salting a few years before his death in 1909, no fewer than twenty are Canton stoneware.

The ivory white Ting and its cousin Ying Ch'ing were also made in the south around the site now known as Ching-tê-chên, a town that since the Ming dynasty has become the greatest porcelain-producing center of the world. They were made at several other locations south of the Yangtze River as well.

The kilns in the south did not suffer the ravages of the invasion. Worth mentioning here is the Chien ware, consisting mainly of tea bowls with black or brown glaze showing striking patterns resembling hare's fur, partridge feathers, or silvery oil spots. These are great favorites of Japanese collectors, who call them *temmoku,* a name derived from the mountain Tien-mu-shan in Chekiang, whence the Japanese

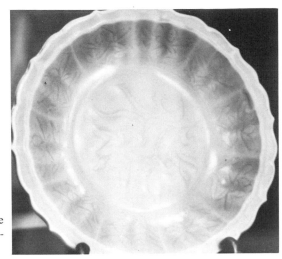

66. Celadon plate, ca. Late Sung. *Hoover Institution, Stanford University*

67. Celadon plate, Lung-ch'üan type; Ch'ing dynasty.

68. Celadon plate decorated in famille rose, ca. 1830.

69. White porcelain vase, shadowy blue where the glaze runs thick. One side shows discoloration, probably due to the fact that it was tipped over during its long period of burial in a tomb. Ying Ch'ing type; possibly late Sung or Yüan period.

Zen monks who came to study Buddhism supposedly first brought these wares back to Japan.

The unique feature of Sung ceramic production is that many kilns were at work at different geographical locations producing equally outstanding wares. Many of these—Kuan, Ju, Lung-ch'üan, Ting, Ying Ch'ing, Chün, Chien—became famous because of their technical excellence, or because they were adopted by the court as palace ware, or were recorded by historians or praised by poets. Although these deservedly attained an exalted place in Chinese ceramic history, there must have been many others—less well known kilns that were arbitrarily merged into one of the above groups, or became provincial and thus were deprecated by early Chinese writers on the subject. In the following dynasties of Yüan, Ming, and Ch'ing, the production of fine porcelains was concentrated at Ching-tê-chên. A Sung piece, on the other hand, could have been made at any one of several known and unknown locations that produced this particular type. Many kilns in the north presumably were still in operation after the court fled south, but written records are lacking. To further the complication, such famous wares as Kuan and Ting were much copied in later ages. Our far-from-complete knowledge is also often subject to revision. When faced with a unique or unfamiliar piece purported to be of this period, experts are sometimes helpless.

70. Incised floral design is faintly visible under celadon glaze on this melon-shaped winepot. Koryŏ dynasty. Korea. Ca. eleventh–twelfth century. *Stanford University Museum*

It is interesting to note that the greatest oriental ceramics were produced from the eleventh through the thirteenth century. While the Sung Chinese were scoring their ceramic triumphs, they had worthy competitors in the Korean potters, who made the famous Koryŏ celadon with its incised decorations or inlaid designs of different colored clays. The glaze, a subtle bluish or greenish color, crackled or crazed. Worth remembering is that Korean celadons are almost always crackled; Chinese celadons are sometimes crackled and sometimes not; Japanese celadons are not crackled. The flowering of Korean ceramics was all too short, and the Mongol conquest brought on a severe decline. If it were not for a report made by a Chinese official who visited Korea at that time and lavished praise upon Koryŏ celadons, and the later discoveries by systematic excavations, the world would have been ignorant of this great Korean achievement.

The Mongol conquest ended the enfeebled Southern Sung dynasty and the classical or middle period of Chinese ceramic history. In the short Mongol (Yüan) dynasty, no ware except perhaps the Shu-fu or palace ware achieved distinction. But the Mongols did introduce from the Near East the technique of underglaze cobalt blue (known as Mohammedan blue) decoration, and perhaps from Korea the underglaze copper red decoration. When the Ming dynasty overthrew the Mongols, Chinese potters were eagerly waiting to stage a comeback.

The Modern Period

The modern age extends from about 1400 to the present day. The body became ever whiter and more compact and translucent. It could be made as thin as eggshell, or "bodiless" so to speak. A transparent glaze was now preferred, to let the beauty of the body show through. Whereas the decoration on Sung wares was limited mostly to incised and pressed designs, thus giving the heavily and sleekly glazed stonewares the carved-jade look, the modern age of Ming and Ch'ing is primarily noted for painted decoration both underglaze and overglaze. For the beginner, a word is necessary to explain the difference.

A piece of modern porcelain is covered or protected by a coat of hard transparent or translucent glaze. To fuse this glaze to the body, it has to be fired at a very high temperature, about 1,300° C. Decorations can be applied directly to the body, then glazed and fired, and the product is finished. However, only cobalt blue and copper red can stand this high temperature, and copper red is difficult to manage. It is necessary to prevent it from coming out too early during the firing (and changing into an undesirable brown or black) by reducing the oxygen

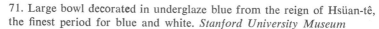

71. Large bowl decorated in underglaze blue from the reign of Hsüan-tê, the finest period for blue and white. *Stanford University Museum*

72. Bowl, blue and white. Late Ming or early Ch'ing.

73. Jar decorated with underglaze blue and overglaze enamels in the style called contrasting or competing colors; ca. seventeenth century. *Stanford University Museum*

in the kiln during the firing. Of course the Chinese had their pet secret formulas: Some potters added powdered precious stones, believing they would enhance the red color. Others added the urine of a small boy to the mixture, reasoning that since it was the quintessence of "Yang," or male, and red was also "Yang," or male, the color could thus be strengthened.

Another method of decoration was by applying enamel colors over the glaze. But since such enamels cannot withstand the high temperature needed to fuse the glaze, the body and glaze must be fired first, either entirely undecorated or decorated only partly in underglaze blue as in Tou Ts'ai (competing colors).

After the first firing at high temperature, the enamels are applied and the piece is refired at a lower temperature to fix them to the glaze. Sometimes enamels are applied over unglazed biscuit, as they are in the

74. Pair of jars decorated with famille verte enamels. They are marked K'ang-hsi but are perhaps later. Height 14½″, diameter 10″.

75. Flask decorated with famille verte enamels, seventeenth or eighteenth century.

76. Jar decorated with famille verte enamels on an oatmeal crackled ground; height 11¼″. Ca. 1900.

77. Three-color ware—green, yellow, and aubergine enamels on biscuit. The front of the bowl is decorated with butterflies on yellow ground.

three-color ware. Without a hard glaze to act as a reflecting surface behind the enamels, a softer effect is achieved.

The question may be asked: Since underglaze colors are difficult to manage and limited in range, then why use them at all? Enamels chip and wear off easily, but underglaze colors are protected by the glaze and so are not subject to wear. There is also the fact that the more difficult a thing is to achieve, the more it is valued. Hence the connoisseur prizes underglaze decoration very highly. However, as the range of enamel colors became almost unlimited during the Ch'ing dynasty, overglaze decoration tended to displace the underglaze type. From the eighteenth century on, underglaze decoration appeared on either fine expensive porcelains or low-priced coarse peasant wares where a few daubs of grayish blue served as the only embellishment.

The early Ming period was another era of great ceramic achievement. It reminds us of the T'ang dynasty. There was a spirit of freedom and a desire for experiment. The underglaze blue and red of the Hsüan-tê period was never surpassed. The charm of the Ch'êng-hua enameled porcelain—the three-color and the five-color, with green, yellow, turquoise, aubergine, and tomato red enamels, sometimes kept within bounds by methods reminiscent of the T'ang technique—was lost when overglaze enamels became sophisticated during the Ch'ing dynasty.

78. On the reverse of No. 77 are yellow and green enameled five-clawed dragons (incised in the biscuit) on a black ground. Incised mark of K'anghsi, and probably of the period.

79. Vase of three-color ware with raised biscuit design; ca. 1880.

80. Jar and brush-washer, three-color ware with raised biscuit design. Ca. 1880 or later.

81. Tea jar with matte brownish black raised floral pattern over a creamy white body. Late nineteenth century.

The porcelain industry was now concentrated at Ching-tê-chên. However, several unique types of ceramics made at other locations also deserve notice:

Blanc de chine. This ivory white porcelain made in Tê-hua, Fukien, was the rage among Western collectors nearly a century ago, and it has never lost its appeal. It is so fine that it is difficult to tell where the compact white paste ends and the unctuous glaze begins. The rare Ming pieces, such as figurines, teapots, and cups, have a warm ivory tone; the modern products are either too white, too gray, or too pink. The difference between blanc de chine and white porcelain is that the former shows no greenish or bluish tinge, but white porcelain often has a slight green color where the glaze runs thick. It must be mentioned that many modern imitations are now being made in the Far East, both in Hong Kong and in Japan.

Yi-hsing ware. A hard stoneware made in a small town not far from Shanghai. It is often unglazed, and the color of the body ranges from light buff to deep brown and reddish purple. However, its lack of bright color helps set off its nearly perfect shape and form. Teapots are the chief items, and a collector can own a hundred of them without finding two duplicates because of their great variety. These teapots are small according to Western standards, and are often mistakenly called winepots. But they were intended as personal teapots. People in Yi-hsing spent many hours a day in the teahouses transacting business, settling disputes, or just meeting and chatting with friends, and regular

82. Pair of Kwan-yin, blanc de chine; height 11″. Ca. 1900.

83. Fish in a basket of pierced work (devil's work). Off-white color; glaze has small, faint crackle. Nineteenth century.

84. Yi-hsing teapot, decorated with various kinds of fruits, nuts, and seeds to go with tea drinking, has a reddish brown unglazed stoneware body. Ca. 1910. The manufacture of this complicated style (the seeds in the lotus pod move freely) apparently was given a new impetus when Stephen W. Bushell illustrated it in his book on Chinese art in 1904.

85. Yi-hsing teapot and cups in light buff color.

86. Yi-hsing teapot on the left has enameled decorations and was made for export. The Chinese prefer these wares without enameling.

customers preferred to bring their own favorite teapots and often their own tea leaves; the teahouse had only to supply boiling water. No teacups were needed, since the spouts of these pots were designed for easy sipping. As a man sipped he would constantly rub the teapot with his hands. After years of such fondling, the pots would acquire a smooth, oily sheen and were greatly treasured.

Fatshan or Shekwan ware. A descendant of Chün ware. Its most prominent features are the hard red or gray stoneware body, and the

87. Planter in the style of Ming three-color ware. Fatshan ware, ca. 1850.

88. Canton pottery fruit glazed in charming old-fashioned green and blushing pink. These items are selling now at unbelievably high prices.

89. Straw yellow wall vases with basket-weave decoration each having a crab and a snail on the shoulder. They can be put together to make one standing vase. Crabs are blue and green; snails, matte brown black.

90. Canton pottery planter with birds and lichee fruit. Ca. 1910.

91. Canton pottery wall vase in polychrome enamels. Ca. 1910.

rich flambé glazes of streaking red, blue, green, white, or brown. A vast
quantity of this ware was exported to the United States—human figures,
vases of all types (some showing Western influence), flowerpots, plant-
ers, animals, birds, and particularly ducks.

When the Manchus took over the nation and established the Ch'ing
dynasty, the emperors K'ang-hsi, Yung-chêng, and Ch'ien-lung were
ardent admirers of Chinese art and culture. The court appointed several
dedicated supervisors to oversee the production of porcelain, and it was
through their devotion that it attained a peak of elegance and dazzling
beauty. The Ch'ing period represents the culmination of Chinese ceramic art. Perhaps we can compare it to the summer season when "hundreds of flowers bloom." The greatest achievement was in the field of
overglaze enamels, which included all colors and all their subtle gradations. This enamel decoration was divided according to a none-too-
precise tradition into (1) famille verte—predominantly green with iron
red, aubergine, and other colors to complement the green; (2) famille
noire—famille-verte-type enamels on black ground; (3) famille jaune—
famille verte on yellow ground; and (4) famille rose—carmine or rose
pink, opaque white, green, and other colors to achieve a softer effect.

Imperial art also began to contribute its services, and we see on
great vases—vases are the aristocrats of Chinese porcelain—
landscapes, birds, and flowers, and genre paintings that can

92. Canton pottery wall vase in poly-chrome enamels. Ca. 1910.

93. Canton pottery figurines of the God of the Sun (*right*) and the Goddess of the Moon (*left*). Ca. 1900.

95. Canton pottery figurines of young Chinese scholars; height 10¾".
Ca. 1900.

◄

94. Canton pottery statuette of Confucius in polychrome enamels; height
10¾". Ca. 1900

96. Plate decorated in famille verte enamels with good artwork. Late eighteenth or early nineteenth century.

97. Plate decorated in famille verte enamels with good artwork. Late eighteenth or early nineteenth century.

98. Plate decorated with superb artwork; diameter 9¾". Ca. 1945.

99. Plate decorated with superb artwork: diameter 9¾". Ca. 1945.

100. Plate decorated with superb art-work; diameter 9¾". Ca. 1945.

101. Plate decorated with superb art-work; diameter 9¾". Ca. 1945.

stand on their own as art. Indeed, the material was worthy of the work of the best artists. The paste was refined to a milky whiteness and a slight tinge of green was imparted by the glaze, which was applied with such skill that very little of the Ming undulating look remained. The potting was firm, sure, and thin. Small wonder that Ch'ing porcelain should be so dazzling in beauty—a fine specimen often passed through the hands of seventy craftsmen and artists.

In the field of blue and white, many authorities consider the K'ang-hsi specimens as superior to those of the Ming period. From the technical point of view, the deep and resonant cobalt blue, the precision and evenness of application, together with the refined paste and firm potting, certainly justify this view.

For connoisseurs who wanted only one color at one time, the Sung glazes were revived and old pieces were sent from the palace to be used as models. It is sometimes difficult to tell the copies from the old. Many monochrome glazes of great beauty were also perfected: sang de boeuf in its many variations, apple green, clair de lune, peach bloom, and mirror black. A vase with any of these glazes is indeed an aristocrat of aristocrats.

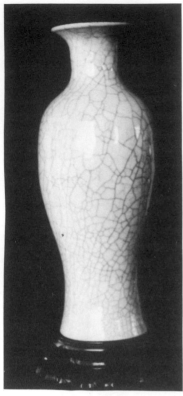

103. Stoneware vase with small (fish-roe type) crackle.

102. Vase with thick grayish white glaze and large (crab's claw type) crackle. Ca. 1880.

Export Wares

The export of porcelain was greatly expanded during the Ch'ing dynasty. Even though these wares were of poor quality, and were often gaudily decorated to cover up the defective body, it was through them that the West learned to know Chinese porcelain. Early export items such as the "Jesuit China" and armorial porcelains have become rare collectors' items, but many of the commoner types listed below are much more available. As required by United States law, any exported to the United States after 1891 were marked "China," or "Made in China." Of course unmarked pieces were brought back by missionaries, businessmen, and tourists as personal property.

1. Famille rose porcelains decorated in Canton. Purists make a fine distinction between "rose Canton," with floral designs, and "rose medallion," with figures in mandarin clothes or with other motifs

painted inside a frame or medallion; and we have been sternly reminded by staunch loyalists not to confuse the one with the other. Actually, they are all gaudy, overdecorated, and often vulgar, and certainly not worth this exercise in hairsplitting. Recently these types have begun to be exported again. They carry marks such as "Japanese porcelain hand decorated in Hong Kong." The marks can be removed easily with fin-

104. Covered jar or vase, rose Canton type. Ca. 1880.

105. Export famille rose porcelain plate (rose Canton). Ca. 1900.

106. Plates of export famille rose porcelain (rose Canton). Ca. 1900.

107. Richly decorated famille rose porcelain related to the rose Canton type. *Top*: Butterflies and cabbage. *Bottom*: Roosters.

gernail polish remover or scouring powder. But you can still tell the difference. The new pieces are brighter in color, and the pink enamel has less shading. The porcelain is whiter and more uniform and shows fewer impurities. The glaze is even and shows no pitting or undulations. Finally, if you run your fingers around the foot ring, you will feel that the new ones are very smooth whereas the old ones often feel sandy and rough. The so-called "complete service" of old rose Canton sold on today's market often includes new replacements. Buyers should examine each piece carefully.

2. Restaurant or "chop suey dishes." These have a certain charm, but they are coarser, heavier, and less finished, though more virile in shape and form, than rose Canton. They are either decorated on both sides or have one side in monochrome yellow or green. The enamels in the floral designs were applied so heavily that they stand out like gems.

3. Export blue and white wares are differentiated into blue Canton and blue Nanking, again a fine distinction. Both were manufactured at Ching-tê-chên. The patterns resemble blue willowware, and the blue has a grayish cast.

108. Blue and white dishes of the rice pattern. Rice-size holes were cut in the biscuit and covered only with greenish glaze. The popular belief that rice grains were imbedded in the biscuit and then allowed to be burned out in the kiln, leaving only a film of glaze, is unfounded.

109. Other items in the rice pattern, some with iron red and gilding over or around the blue designs. Both the Chinese and Japanese have made this type of ware. The Chinese products have a distinctive greenish glaze and are a thinner porcelain.

110. Chop suey (restaurant) dishes with thickly piled-on enamels in different color combinations. (Recent imports use very little enamel, applied thinly like pigment.) Ca. 1900–1920.

111. Household ware of porcelain with polychrome enamels. The large butterfly is black. Ca. 1920.

112. Export porcelain in underglaze blue (blue Nanking type); eighteenth or nineteenth century.

113. Fo lions (or Fo dogs) in almost identical peacock blue glaze. The left one was made in Italy and is dated 1815, but the right is Chinese, 1900.

114. The Happy Buddha (Pu-tai). Famille rose porcelain. Ca. 1900.

115. The roly-poly Pu-tai is a lover of children, and vice versa. Ca. 1900.

116. The God of Longevity (Shou Shing). Famille rose porcelain. Ca. 1900.

117. Pair of porcelain cranes; height 12″. Ca. 1900.

118. Porcelain vase in blue and white with dark brown bands. The mark of Ch'êng-hua is scratched in a patch of brown glaze. The vase has an odd, irregular crackle. (Many of this type were made in Japan.)

119. Vase with brownish glaze and oatmeal crackle, decorated with ancient battle scenes in brick red and other dark, unpleasant-looking polychrome enamels. Brown dressing on lip, shoulder, and band above foot. Ch'êng-hua mark under the foot. (Some of this type are Chinese, but most are of Japanese make.)

Japan and Korea

Japan entered the field of porcelain making rather late, not until the sixteenth century. However, even with such a comparatively short period of production there is a problem of identification, which is complicated by the fact that many kilns were operating at the same time and by the potters' practice of purloining guarded secrets from one another under the patronage of different jealous local rulers. There is no extensive record of early porcelain production. Controversy abounds. Take, for instance, the case of old Kutani, or ko-Kutani. There has never been any standard as to when the making of old Kutani ended and the new began. One Japanese authority flatly states that there is no such thing as old Kutani.

The Japanese themselves preferred pottery, but the case of pottery is still more complicated. For one thing, the kilns were more numerous. Some were operated by a single artist-potter such as Kenzan, whose ware bears his signature; some by one family, as in the case of Raku. Or a ware may have become famous merely because it received the praise of a certain teamaster. Such celebrated names as Seto, Oribe, Raku, Imbe, and Karatsu may not be familiar to the beginning collector, but no one can miss the rustic charm and poetic appeal of Japanese pottery. It has certainly exerted great influence on the collegiate potters of many American campuses.

A large quantity of pottery was also manufactured for export, and this type was decorated rather ornately to suit Western taste. The products of the Satsuma factories, richly and often elegantly decorated in brocade patterns on a soft creamy crackled ground, enjoyed great popularity in the West during the nineteenth and early twentieth centuries. Export pottery wares were also made at Kyoto, Tokyo, and many other locations. Unfortunately, the term Satsuma came to be used by collectors as the catchall for all Japanese ceramic exports, including the monstrosities known as the Nagasaki wares, which are examples of unbelievably bad taste.

Another favorite of Western collectors is the export porcelain Imari—named for the seaport from which the wares were shipped. However, authorities now tend to believe that most export Imari wares were actually shipped from Nagasaki. Made at Arita, one of Japan's great

120. Design of flowering camellia and pine in the snow on this jar is done in enamels of brick red, green, and white. By Kenzan (1664–1743), Japan. *Stanford University Museum*

121. Satsuma pottery vase with finely crackled, creamy glaze is ornately decorated with enamels and gilding. Ca. 1880.

122. Satsuma-type pottery vase decorated with children and unrelated motifs in a crowded design. Ca. 1900.

123. Pottery teapot with buff crackled glaze and decoration in green, red, yellow, and turquoise enamels. Signed Kinkousan.

124. Imari bowl, ca. nine-
teenth century. *Dr. and
Mrs. Marvin Hockabout
Collection*

125. Imari plate, ca. nine-
teenth century. *Dr. and
Mrs. Marvin Hockabout
Collection*

porcelain manufacturing centers, these wares were lavishly decorated
with rapidly drawn peonies, chrysanthemums, fish, and figures, with
brocade border patterns, in color combinations of underglaze blackish
violet blue and overglaze enamels of orange, red, green, and gold.
Imari ware has a great deal of exotic charm, and it became so popular
in the West that at one time the Chinese copied the designs on their
export porcelains. (These became known as Chinese Imari.) Its wide
variety of shapes and forms contributed to the popularity of Imari.
Marks serve only as decorations, such as the character "fuku" (good
luck) or the Chinese reign mark of Ch'êng-hua of the Ming dynasty.
Blue-and-white was also exported. It often copied Chinese Ming motifs
and had Ming marks hastily and haphazardly written in.

To connoisseurs, Arita is best remembered for producing two of
the most celebrated wares of Japanese porcelain: Nabeshima and Kakiemon.

Nabeshima is a very fine porcelain made exclusively for the local
noble house. Its skillful designs often extended to the edge. The colors
included blue-and-white, as well as a combination of any of the following: green, orange, red, and pale yellow enamels, and underglaze blue.
Its identifying features are its unique shape—a hybrid between a plate
and a bowl, the coin marks on the back, and the comb mark on the

126. Nabeshima ware. The shape is often a cross between a plate and a bowl. Decoration is in underglaze blue with overglaze red and light blue green enamels.

127. The reverse of the Nabeshima dish in No. 126. The comb mark on the high foot rim and the coin design on the back are typical of this fine ware.

128. Kakiemon bowl. *Stanford University Museum*

129. Old Kutani bottle-shaped vase; early seventeenth century. *Stanford University Museum*

130. Kutani or Arita bottle-shaped porcelain vase; eighteenth century.

strong and wide foot-rim; but above all it is distinguished for extremely fine quality and workmanship. Nabeshima was never made for sale, and today it is priced deservedly high.

Kakiemon wares include some of the finest porcelain ever made in Japan. The decorations were done in various combinations of the following: underglaze blue, and enamels of green, blue, turquoise, yellow, and the unique persimmon red. Stylized Chinese motifs were often used, and the workmanship was skillful and meticulous. The outstanding features of this ware were much copied by early European potters. Kakiemon wares are also among the highest-priced collectors' items today, and are extremely difficult to find.

Another important group of porcelains was produced by the Kutani factories. The Kutani porcelain industry was started by craftsmen who first learned the technique at Arita. However, their product soon developed a distinctive character and style, notably free and powerful brushwork and its use of empty spaces. The enamel colors consisted of heavy brownish red, muddy yellow, and intense green. The old green Kutani (ao-Kutani) is considered by some authorities as one of the most exciting types of porcelain made in Japan.

Recently, people have begun collecting Japanese porcelain made from early in the 1900s down to about 1950, the reason being that, although it is quite plentiful now, it will become increasingly scarce one day, following the course of natural depletion. These wares were made exclusively for the Western market, and since Western motifs were used, they are therefore different from the Imari type. Often the earlier wares are marked "Nippon"; then "Japan" appeared with increasing frequency as "Nippon" gradually came to be used less and less often. During the short period of American occupation, they were marked "Made in Occupied Japan." These fine-quality porcelains were made by several large manufacturers. Perhaps the best known is Noritake china made by the Nihon Toki Kaisha at Nagoya. The company has produced porcelain since 1904 and still holds a large part of the Western market.

Finally, a word about Korean porcelain of the Yi dynasty: The Mongol and Japanese invasions caused a serious deterioration in porcelain production. The material remained coarse. The decoration, in blue-and-white or iron brown, was sparse but spontaneous. What it lacked in elegance and refinement was perhaps made up by the strength and vitality of the potting and the free calligraphic painting. The quantity made was so small that rarely does one find a Korean specimen on the open market today.

131. Japanese decorated celadon saucers. The decorations, in pink, dark green, and white, are applied both under and over the glassy, light green glaze. Note the peculiar blunt grass blades and leaves. This type of seemingly unnatural reverse stroke was used perhaps because of the need for speed in decorating.

132. Modern Japanese celadon bowl. The impressed pattern and glaze are perfect—too perfect.

133. Modern bowls. The one at left is marked "Made in Kiangsi, Ching-tê-chên." The other is marked "Made in Occupied Japan." They appear identical in paste, potting, shape, form, glaze, and even the colors of the enamels. Without the marks no expert could tell the countries of origin.

134. Modern Japanese porcelain plate decorated with theatre masks, musical instruments, brocade patterns of polychrome enamels, and gilding.

135. Decoration on this Korean wine bottle is carved through the white slip that covers the brown body. Yi dynasty, ca. fifteenth century. *Stanford University Museum*

136. Selection of Nippon (*top row*) and Noritake wares (*bottom row*), ca. 1920 except for the vase, which is post-World War II.

Advice for the Ceramics Collector

Collecting oriental porcelain is a difficult endeavor. Prices for even the seventeenth- or eighteenth-century pieces are prohibitively high. Fakes abound, but modern science has given us new detection devices. Chemical analysis of shards excavated from known and unknown kiln sites and the recently invented thermoluminescence test,* for instance, have rendered great service to museums. Perhaps someday this type of service will become available to collectors. Still, scientific tests are only tools. They cannot take the place of knowledge, nor of the taste to distinguish the outstanding and the beautiful from the mediocre. Our knowledge in this field is not complete and it never can be. Problems of dating and attribution will never be entirely solved. Occasionally pieces made by obscure kilns many centuries ago will wander into the market, and when they do, a man of integrity can only admit his ignorance.

However, when such pieces are brought to an appraiser, what does he say? All too often he will adopt the convenient attitude of the geography teacher who, when asked during a job interview whether he taught that the earth is round or flat, replied, "I can teach either way." When money is offered, there are at least a few appraisers who are ready to authenticate anything. This is how fakes and doubtful pieces attain the exalted position of genuine Sung or Ming specimens.

The collector fortunate enough to know an expert on oriental ceramics can seek his help, though expertise in this field is only one man's opinion against another's, and there is often disagreement. To err is human, and in this difficult field experts err frequently.

The collector can of course develop his own expertise by extensive reading, visiting museums, and examining authenticated specimens, as we have already explained. Each period had its unique styles, shapes, forms, glazes, enamels, motifs, and paste, and a combination of all these gives a piece the look of its period. In time, after a good deal of careful observation and persistent study, the collector reaches a point where he has developed a sixth sense and can say, "This can't be a Ming piece," or "Don't ask me why, but I feel sure this is not genuine."

Sometimes, however, one can rely on quite obvious features. For instance, when a seller labels as Ming a piece that shows carmine or rose pink enamel in the decoration, the well-informed collector is not

---

* Based upon the fact that ancient pottery glows when heated, whereas fakes do not.

fooled. He knows that rose pink did not come into existence until the late K'ang-hsi period. Therefore a good rule to follow is: Look for what *shouldn't* be there.

Quite often it can be costly to place too much dependence on the obvious. Reign marks are a good example. The dealer or seller will often point out a reign mark to prove the authenticity of his piece. "It has a K'ang-hsi mark at the bottom," he will boast; ergo, it is three hundred years old!

Can reign marks be trusted? The answer is No.

The use of reign marks had not become fashionable during the Sung period, but from the Ming dynasty onward, they began to appear regularly. Ming marks are sometimes on the necks of articles and sometimes under the foot; Ch'ing marks are almost always under the foot.

137. Pair of teacups, blue and white. Mark: "Hsüan-tê period made." The word "Tê" can be written either with or without the horizontal stroke (see arrow on table at right). However, authentic "Hsüan-tê" marks are almost never written with this stroke. These fine cups whose marks do contain the stroke should be assigned to the early Ch'ing period. Also, the bamboo mat design around the top edge did not become popular until the K'ang-hsi period.

The wares of any period that became classic were much copied in later ages, not only in shape and form but also in design and decoration, including the reign marks. The Chinese were not the only potters to follow this custom. The Japanese too added all sorts of Chinese reign marks to pieces using Chinese motifs.

The wares of the classical periods are, to name a few, the underglaze blues and reds of the Hsüan-tê reign; the overglaze enameled wares of the C'hêng-hua reign; the monochromes, the famille verte, and the underglaze blues of the K'ang-hsi, and the famille rose of the Ch'ien-lung periods. These wares were much imitated and the reign marks freely copied. Naturally, all the Sung wares rank at the very top of this prestigious group.

The Ch'ien-lung style, meaning finely drawn famille rose decorations on thin, milky white body, remains popular today—the most recent "Made in Japan and Decorated in Hong Kong" copies carry Ch'ien-lung marks.

There are of course authentic marks; most of the items marked Tao-kuang (1821–1850) or Kuang-hsü (1874–1908) can be considered authentic. Many K'ang-hsi porcelains are unmarked, since an edict forbade using the emperor's name on porcelain. The edict resulted from the superstitious belief that if the emperor's name appeared on these wares and was shattered many times—indeed, thousands of times —a day all over the nation, it would surely bring him bad luck. There was also the consideration that these vessels might be used to contain filthy things, thus befouling the emperor's name. The rule seems to have been relaxed or disregarded during the later part of the reign.

In short, a reign mark can mean only that the piece is no older than the mark indicates. In most cases, it should be utterly ignored.*

Other extraneous frills should be disregarded. Do not be impressed, for instance, by a glass-topped, silk-lined, custom-made case in which a supposed "treasure" snugly rests. In China, even a 25-cent sandalwood fan came in a silk-lined, custom-made glass case.

---

* Collectors are often puzzled by the double ring of underglaze blue under many of the vases. This fact can be explained as follows: A piece of Ch'ing porcelain passed through many hands before firing. There was a man to make the double rings and another to write in the reign marks. There were times when the old emperor had just died and a successor had not ascended the throne, and so the ring was left blank. Or the artist (a trained calligrapher hard to replace) might have been ill, but the production line still had to keep on moving. Or the kiln manager might decide to save money by eliminating the job since it wasn't mandatory to put reign marks on every piece of porcelain.

138. Front of a large plate decorated with five bats in iron red.

139. The reverse of No. 138 is decorated in enamels with imperial dragons and phoenixes. Mark of Tao-kuang (1821–1850), and of the period. Perhaps palace ware.

The best tools a collector can use are his knowledge, his discerning eyes, his sensitive fingers, and his logic, but not his ears.

Theoretically, a faker has at his disposal the techniques to make any kind of imitation from the T'ang dynasty to the Ch'ien-lung period, since these old techniques are still known. Quite often his imitations will fool 90 percent of the collectors and dealers, and even some museums; and that's good enough for him. To fool the other 10 percent, who are top scholars and experts, he would have to go to too great an expense. Kilns are built differently today and work more efficiently, and raw materials come in a more refined state. Since the faker wants to make easy money by utilizing existing facilities and easily available material, he will not go to the expense of building an archaic kiln or importing cobalt blue from the Middle East just to fool that other 10 percent.

Often the faker will seek only to please the eye, and will fail to satisfy the sense of touch, and often the area under and around the foot will betray his effort. That is why old-time Chinese connoisseurs always closed their eyes and felt a piece with their trained, sensitive fingers, particularly around the foot area. The faker may rub pot grease and ashes into the rough foot ring, but these can be easily removed with a little soap and water. The genuine patina that gives a piece an authentic look takes years to form. It cannot be achieved overnight. When a piece was buried for even a century or two, there was a subtle change in the body, the glaze, and the area where the two meet.

The beginner should never be cocksure just because he has read two or three books on ceramics. In China there is a saying, "When a person has studied for three years, he feels he knows the whole world; but after he has studied another three years, he feels he can't even take one small step." Alexander Pope put it more aptly, "A little learning is a dangerous thing." If a beginner thinks he has found an old authentic treasure, he should forget it if he has to pay the price of an old authentic piece. But he can take a chance if the price is no more than that of, say, a good modern copy—99 percent of the so-called T'ang, Sung, and Ming specimens and perhaps 90 percent of the K'ang-hsi and Ch'ien-lung pieces on the market today are copies anyway.

However, a beginner should not therefore shy away from this most complicated and uncertain department of all oriental arts. A person who is careful and sharp of observation and who cares to develop his knowledge will be rewarded most handsomely. One infallible rule to follow is to look for intrinsic artistic merit regardless of how old the piece may be. Artistic merit (in shape, form, body, glaze, decoration) should always be the first and last consideration. The landscape of the Orient is full of old things. An object can be truly five hundred years old, but still be a piece of junk that happens to be old.

Once a dealer showed us a tubular vase with a crudely molded dragon on it. It was partly covered by a turquoise-colored glaze. He said we could have it for a drastically reduced price: $100. It was Ming all right. The roadside shrines in China were full of such stuff. This one had apparently been yanked out from the stone altar where it was cemented—we could see the discolored plaster on the bottom. But why should anybody pay $100 for a piece of junk—even if it is Ming junk?

For the person who wants to collect simply for fun, we recommend that, instead of paying high prices for the current favorites of the collecting world, such as rose Canton and Imari, he pay attention to the following categories:

1. *Ch'ien-lung-style porcelains.* These have a thin, milky white body with paintings in delicate famille rose colors. They have Ch'ien-

lung marks in iron red, blue enamel, or underglaze blue. The marks, of course, should be disregarded. An eight- or nine-inch vase can be bought for about $20; an overdecorated, coarse rose Canton vase of the same size will cost around $35.

2. *Yi-hsing teapots.*   These beautiful stonewares are much under-rated. They can be bought on the market for as little as $8.

3. *Containers* for herb liquor, soy sauce, pickled ginger, and various vegetables. They are made of both porcelain and stoneware. The porcelain type, such as the blue and white prunus tea jars, are selling at very high prices. But the unpretentious stoneware types, with a variety of glazes from white, green, brown, mahogany, and blue black to black, have a truly robust and antique look. They have been made the same way since the Sung or T'ang dynasties. Many of the older pieces were painted over with morning glories and grape designs when there was a fad here to redecorate oriental containers. The paint can be easily removed. These containers will make a display of rustically beautiful pieces that are identical with Sung or Ming specimens in every way except age. Pay attention to those with interesting colors and patterns such as hare's fur or silvery oil spots.

4. *Blue-and-white porcelains.*   These items are high-priced. Perversely, crude coolie wares of coarse paste and impure glaze, decorated perfunctorily by untrained hands in grayish blue, sell for high prices because they look very old. But, strangely, quality pieces of fine decoration in resonant blue over translucent paste often sell no higher because they do not look so old. Sometimes, they are simply dismissed as modern Japanese copies.

The Japanese made and exported a large quantity of porcelain in blue-and-white. Much of it copied Ming motifs and is complete with Ming reign marks. It is difficult for beginning collectors to tell the copies from the authentic pieces, particularly because during the early days the Japanese imported cobalt blue from China. However, there are these differences: Japanese decorations often show exaggerated brush-strokes. The leaves are very blunt. The grass blades, instead of tapering at the ends, often are also blunt because Japanese decorators executed their strokes from the tip to the stem. Human figures, whether officials or scholars, often betray some irrelevant movement; the Chinese, on the other hand, preferred to show figures in serene and dignified poses. Chinese porcelain often has a slight greenish tinge in the glaze; Japanese porcelain is lighter, either very white or slightly grayish, and has, as one authority puts it, "the muslin look." That is, the overall look reminds one of the texture of that fabric.

140. Eggshell porcelain lamp with polychrome enamel diaper pattern on yellow ground. White reserve panels are decorated with katydid and chrysanthemums in famille rose enamels. Ch'ien-lung style; ca. 1900.

141. Ch'ien-lung style vase showing scholar and his attendant cultivating bamboo on a conspicuously soft green glaze.

142. Container for Chinese liquor is porcelain decorated with red and yellow enamels and gilding; ca. 1900.

143. Plate in mille-fleur pattern, famille rose over a black ground. Marked Ch'ien-lung, but perhaps later.

144. Both these vases have cobalt blue background with the prunus design left in white. The one on the left is dark violet blue; the other is sapphire blue. Both are middle or late nineteenth century. *Left*: height 11¾"; *right*: height 9½".

145. Provincial ware found at an 1870 railroad campsite.

146. Porcelain household ware in underglaze blue and green, ca. 1900. (Recent imports have a more uniform body and glaze.)

147. Japanese blue and white vase using Ming motif. The Chinese would paint the figures in more serene and more dignified poses. Otherwise, it is very hard to tell the difference.

148. Japanese pieces with printed underglaze blue design. (Oriental porcelains with printed designs are not valued very highly.)

The Japanese also made a great deal of blue-and-white porcelain with printed patterns. To the connoisseur of oriental porcelains, those with printed or stenciled designs are not acceptable, although relief patterns, whether incised or impressed, do not make too much difference. Under a magnifying glass, a printed pattern looks fuzzy, or as if made up of dotted lines.

Let us get back at last to the question raised at the beginning of this chapter—the possibility of stumbling on a really valuable find. There are always surprises, if you keep looking. For instance, two years ago we saw a few oriental antiques displayed in the window of a little dress shop. Among them was a small peach-bloom vase, and we asked to see it. The price was only $175, but the color was poor. We decided against it. The vase was gone in a few days. Later, we noticed in a large antique store a vase of comparable quality (it could have been the same one) priced at $1,900. Did we pass up a treasure? Perhaps. But we are collecting for fun, and we could never like a peach-bloom vase with an unpleasant brownish cast.

Recently, however, we noticed a large old lamp in a junk store. The vase-shaped body was covered with a thick coat of white paint, which had turned yellowish, but the faint ridges showing under the paint convinced us that it was an oriental piece. Scratches on the paint indicated the color was black underneath. With the aid of a pocket magnifying glass, we could see that the black glaze had microscopic wrinkles running from the top to the bottom, a sign that the glaze was thick and perhaps consisted of several coats. The brown color under the lip further confirmed our suspicions. Hastily we paid the $3 asked for it. Three coats of paint remover later, before our eyes stood a 19-inch K'ang-hsi mirror-black vase worth over $500! And just two weeks before this find, at a flea market we bought a lamp made from a fine 12-inch celadon vase and paid 75¢ for it. So careful scrutiny combined with knowledge and a bit of luck can pay off.

As a matter of fact, most of our finer vases were formerly lamps. In the early 1900s, it was a fad to make lamps out of fine antique vases, which were reasonably priced and easily available. In his book, Warren E. Cox mentions that he turned many fine vases into lamps, some of them specimens of the Sung and Ming periods. We have still to find any like that, but we are looking.

You should too.

PLATE 1. Hanging on the wall is the front of a K'ossu imperial robe, ca. nineteenth century. Beside it hangs a teakwood lantern with jade beads. The table at left bears an archaic bronze kuei, a pottery peach, and a pink-glazed vase. The gourd-shaped vase on the center table is cloisonné. A Japanese porcelain Kannon (Kuan-yin), an archaic bronze mirror, and a Peking glass bowl stand on the table at right. Under the tables are a celadon jar and molded Bodhisattvas. The teakwood tables are carved with bamboo and grape designs.

PLATE 2. *Back row (left to right)*: amethyst jar carved with grapevines and birds; smoky quartz statuette of Bodhidarma (founder of Ch'an Buddhism) on amethyst stand; jade, type Tsung (symbol of earth). *Front row:* jade cup; jade finger citron with "ink-splash" markings; rose quartz Pu-tai; rock crystal Kuan-yin.

PLATE 3. Two horizontal scrolls by Ch'i Pai-shih (1861–1957).

PLATE 4. Birds and flowers by Chang Shu-chi (1900–1958).

PLATE 5. Wood-block print by Hiroshege
(1797–1858).

PLATE 6. Vases that were formerly lamps. *Top (left to right)*: vase with yellow glaze and landscape in reserve panel is marked Chu Jen T'ang, hall name of Yuan Shih-k'ai, whose abortive monarchy lasted only a short time; large, squat famille rose vase; vase with turquoise green glaze and famille rose floral design. *Under the table, back row*: vase with celadon glaze; vase with pink glaze; *front row*: vase with famille rose decoration; famille verte club vase with fine painting; vase with yellow glaze and famille rose design. On either side of table are K'ang-hsi mirror-black vases with the so-called yin (female) and yang (male) shapes.

PLATE 7. Types of decorations and glazes. *Top (left to right)*: underglaze blue decoration; powder blue with gilding; turquoise (peacock blue) glaze with incised decoration. *Bottom*: combination of underglaze red and blue decoration; celadon glaze with pressed design; deep green glaze; mirror-black glaze; deep blue glaze.

PLATE 8. Types of decorations and glazes: *Top (left to right)*: celadon glaze with patch of peach-bloom glaze; red flambé glaze with streaking blue; flambé glaze of blue and green. *Bottom*: teadust glaze; leopard skin, or the so-called egg and spinach glaze of yellow, green, aubergine, and white; sang-de-boeuf glaze, which tends to flow during firing, leaving the neck white.

PLATE 9. Porcelain in Ch'ien-lung style, post-1900. The white, thin, compact porcelain is covered with transparent glaze and delicately painted in famille rose enamels.

PLATE 10. The careful modeling and glazing of these ducks is a testimonial to the Chinese love of domestic animals.

PLATE 11. Chinese pottery crab vases. Small vases, ca. 1900; large one, eighteenth century.

PLATE 12. Containers like these have been made and glazed in the same way since the Sung period. The two large whitish jars, excavated from the site of an 1875 railroad construction camp, could be easily mistaken for Ming jars. The glaze has acquired a slight iridescence, the underglaze blue has run and spread, and the body is discolored.

PLATE 13. Chinese cloisonné. *Top:* vases and a candlestick. *Bottom:* box with Peking opera scene; waterpipe; stirrup; spectacle case.

PLATE 14. Japanese cloisonné of outstanding workmanship.

PLATE 15. Peking glass. *Top (left to right)*: one of a pair of connubial bowls with double happiness mark and the commendation "simulated jade"; snuff bottle, painted inside; bowl carved in high relief; snuff bottle of solid tomato red; peacock green bowl. *Bottom:* cat of milk white glass; cucumber; turnip; jar with blue overlay cut in geometric pattern; red and green peppers; aubergine-colored fish; pink snuff-bottle saucer.

PLATE 16. Chinese glass beads. *Left to right:* blue glass pendant with kingfisher feather trim; cinnamon and green beads with cinnamon drop; three shades of amber tassel beads with feather-trimmed drop; cobalt and sapphire blue with blue tubes and pancake; black glass with good imitation-jade pancake; blue and red beads; deep pink beads with gourd and feather-drop pendant, yellow and orange beads with yellow pancake; green beads with inside-painted lamp finial; beads and pancake of green, red, and white mottled glass; cobalt blue beads with drop of circlets; necklace showing the wide variety of colors available; cranberry red beads with inside-painted finial; porcelaneous beads of blue, white, and red with blue pancake; cloisonné sphere with glass and brass beads; deep amethyst and green beads; green coin-shaped disks from lantern; goldstone and blue beads; red drop with kingfisher-feather trim.

PLATE 17. Chinese embroidery of the Ku hsiu type, noted for its naturalistic style and delicate shading.

PLATE 18. This section of inlaid tray pictures a charming fantasy land in which the Taoist hermit lives with a butterfly and flowers almost as large as human beings, and the peach tree, an important Taoist symbol, bears large fruit though yet in full bloom. Bought for only $1.50, the old tray was worth the time and effort expended in finding large pearl buttons and sanding, incising, and fitting them into place to restore it. (*See* also illustration 248.)

PLATE 19. Ch'i-lin and dragons from an 18 Tong hall hanging are gold-thread laidwo scintillating with tiny mirrors.

CLOISONNÉ, CHAMPLEVÉ, PAINTED ENAMELS

FROM THE BEGINNING OF THE BRONZE AGE, THERE WAS A CONSCIOUS desire to decorate the vessels made of this alloy. The earliest effort was the casting and carving of relief patterns, such as the lai-wen, or thunder pattern, and the T'ao-t'ieh monster masks. Lacquer and pigments were also used as a surface treatment. By the middle and late Chou period, inlay work with silver and gold became popular (Chin-ts'un style). Semiprecious stones were also being used. The hill-type incense burners of the Han dynasty, representing the Taoists' concept of the realm of the immortals, were often aglow with stones. During the T'ang dynasty, repoussé work of silver and gold was used as decoration over bronze mirrors.

Although there is inconclusive evidence that a crude form of cloisonné was made during the T'ang dynasty, this kind of enamel decoration did not start on a large scale until the Ming dynasty. Fine specimens were made as early as the Hsüan-tê reign; however, Chinese sources attribute the beginning of cloisonné work to the Ching-t'ai period, and to this day cloisonné is still known in China as Ching-t'ai blue, the beautiful turquoise blue so typical of the Ming pieces. There is very little doubt that the Ming Chinese learned much of the technique of cloisonné-making from the Mideastern nations.

Cloisonné and champlevé are closely related, but not quite the same. Champlevé work is done by filling in, with enamels, the patterns that are created by casting or chiseling, whereas cloisonné work requires the use of metal ribbons or wires, which are soldered or glued to the metal body, to form the desired patterns. The individual cells or

149. Chinese cloisonné vase with pink plum blossoms on green ground; height 8″. Ca. 1920.

150. Chinese cloisonné ashtrays and cigarette box with polychrome enamels on white ground; ca. 1920.

cloisons then must be repeatedly filled with enamels, fired, sanded, and polished—a much more exacting process and one that often inspired more refined and intricate workmanship.

The cloisonné wares of the Ming period are magnificent, even though the colors are sometimes muddy and run into each other, particularly when the solder melted, rose to the surface, and became mixed with the enamels during the firing. The color range was limited. When a lighter color such as pink was desired, particles of white enamel were mixed with particles of red, and on close inspection the pink has a salami look. These Ming pieces had cast-bronze bodies, and the ribbons or wires were also made of bronze. After the sixteenth century, copper, because of its malleability, began to take the place of bronze.

Better control and better color characterized the pieces made during the Ch'ien-lung period, when the palace had its own atelier. The more finished and refined pieces of Chinese cloisonné were produced during this period. These were ornate and heavily gilded, and many of

152. Japanese cloisonné covered jar of floral design with an overall somber look. Background of reddish brown is sprinkled with gold dust. This is the old type of cloisonné, ca. 1875.

151. Brush holder is Japanese cloisonné over a pottery base. The Seto potters made cloisonné on pottery around 1868. It proved not to be a happy combination, and was discontinued. They used bronze wires and turquoise blue enamel—both unique features of Ming cloisonné. Perhaps they copied directly from Ming specimens.

the fine ones in the form of incense burners, candlesticks, and vases were given to the various temples by the emperor.

The quality of the cloisonné began to deteriorate when the great demand arose for pieces to export to the West. Mass production and careless workmanship resulted in a tremendous quantity of poor-quality products, which were often sold by the pound to Western importers. Holes in the enamel were filled in with wax. Later on, when the wax melted, these unsightly pits reappeared. The collectibles on the market today, such as ashtrays, cigarette boxes, napkin rings, and the like, belong in this class.

Although the magnificence of the best Chinese cloisonné has never been surpassed by that of any other country, the Japanese products are unexcelled in refinement, elegance, and meticulous workmanship. The Japanese began to produce fine cloisonné around 1830, and may or may not have learned the art from the Chinese. Whatever its parent-

153. Large Japanese cloisonné jardiniere and stand with design of purple and white wisteria on a dark blue ground; height 3½'. Ca. 1880.

age, Japanese cloisonné shows many innovations and great technical skill. Many older Japanese pieces were decorated with Chinese motifs, but the transparent enamels, the characteristic reddish brown with a sprinkle of gold, give one a fleeting feeling of somberness and wistfulness that is uniquely Japanese. The achievements of modern Japanese cloisonné art are even more impressive. The decoration has become entirely naturalistic. Often they splash a whole picture, like a painting, against a plain dark background. (In fact, one way to tell whether a piece is Chinese or Japanese is that the Chinese always fill the empty space with key fret, thundercloud, or other patterns, but the Japanese prefer to leave it blank.) The Japanese also applied transparent enamels over silver or aluminum foil with pressed designs as backgrounds. The finest wires were used so that they would appear merely as outlines, like the brushstrokes on oriental paintings, just large enough to give the necessary definition. They employed ceramic as well as metal bases for their work, and made the so-called bodiless pieces (plique à jour), in which the base was withdrawn after the work was finished.

Fine specimens of Japanese cloisonné often bear the signatures of the artists or makers' marks. Chinese cloisonné sometimes bears the Ch'ien-lung reign mark, or the Ching-t'ai and Hsüan-tê marks of the Ming dynasty, or "Made during the great Ming Dynasty." These marks are either incised or in enamel. In any case, collectors should judge a

154. Japanese champlevé vase with archaic Chinese motif; ca. 1880.

155. Japanese bronze vase decorated with a band of champlevé enamels in the middle. Wan-li (1573–1620) mark under foot. Ca. 1900.

piece on its own merit. Reign marks on cloisonné can be faked or put on by incision, or by simply adding another base to the piece.

The Chinese have made little champlevé during recent times. The Japanese, however, produced a great quantity of it during the early part of the century, frequently complete with Ming marks. The enamel decorations often cover the body only partly, sometimes only in a narrow band. Many of these pieces have become lamp bases, and it is not profitable to extract them out of their fixtures as they do make very appropriate heavy and handsome lamps.

156. Japanese bronze vase with a narrow band of champlevé enamels; ca. 1900.

Chinese painted enamels (metal wares coated with an opaque enamel fused by low firing, painted with gay designs, and refired) were called "foreign porcelain" because it was the Jesuit priests who introduced them to China. They were considered gaudy and were not favored by the scholars who dictated tastes. Painted enamels were made both in Peking for the court and around Canton in the south for export. The export items, such as cigarette boxes, napkin rings, ashtrays, and matchboxes, were of very poor quality.

The prices of cloisonné and painted enamels have gone up steeply during the last few years. These fragile objects can suffer damage easily, and most pieces available on the market today show some damage. However, they can be repaired or even restored, using the methods explained in Chapter 15.

Although a few specimens have come out of China recently, they are only a drop compared to the torrent produced during the eighteenth, nineteenth, and early twentieth centuries. The Orient can no longer be expected to continue to supply cheap labor to produce fine handicrafts for the West, and so collectors will do well to save whatever they can find and do all they can in the way of repairs and restoration. The legendary age of Eastern splendor, of clipper ships laden with treasures, will never return again.

157. Chinese enamel vase with reserve panels decorated with bird and
peaches on yellow floral ground; ca.
1900.

158. Stack of four matching Chinese
enamel containers with a cover. The
decoration consists of a floral design
on a pink ground, and landscape
panels. Ca. 1900.

159. Chinese enameled tray is decorated with a floral design on a dark
purple ground and figures in the reserve panel; ca. 1920.

160. Chinese enamel trays.

161. Chinese enamel candleholders.

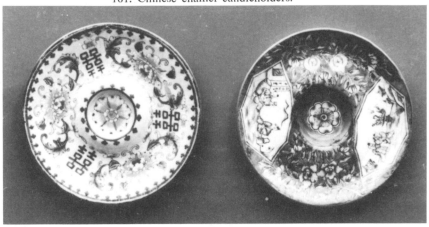

162. Large Chinese enamel plate with pink, green, and yellow floral design on white ground.

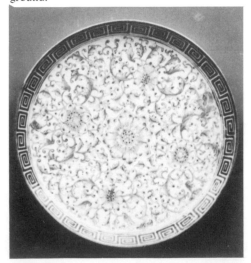

8

PEKING GLASS

"WHAT ARE THOSE BOWLS DOING AT AN ANTIQUE SHOW LIKE THIS? They look almost like the Rice Krispies giveaways I got years ago."

As we made our way through the crowd at a splendid antique show and sale, we could not help but overhear the disparaging remark, and we noted the items referred to. On a back bottom shelf of one of the most lavish displays was a pair of soft blue green glass rice bowls. Not satisfied with dismissing them in such a way, we asked to examine them. Molded in the glass on the bottom of each bowl were tiny Chinese characters that read "Ming-yuan simulated jade," and there was also the double happiness inscription that indicated they were a pair of bridal bowls probably brought from China by a couple who immigrated to this country in the late 1800s. Or perhaps a "picture bride" had brought them with her when she came to meet her husband who had literally "bought" her from her parents through a marriage broker in Canton. The wealthy had jade bridal bowls, but the middle class had to settle for simulated jade or glass. Jade stands for endurance, beauty, and faithfulness in marriage. The glass was no doubt serving in the place of jade, and it had indeed lasted a long time.

These bridal bowls were the first Peking glass objects in our collection. Since then we have had relatively good luck in getting a few more, but they are becoming rare and the price increases constantly.

Inspection of these lovely bowls reveals a simulated fibrous texture that does not just happen; it is caused by too much alkali in the glass mixture. The Chinese deliberately achieve this softest tone of turquoise blue by the use of copper in a deoxidizing flux in the presence of an excess of niter. (Niter, found in a natural state in Shantung Province in great quantities, was the source of the alkali.) The bowls have added foot rims, which were ground to make them stand level. One bowl differs slightly from the other in weight and size, which indicates that even though they were originally molded, considerable handwork was done on each one. So much for the "Rice Krispies" bowls.

Collectors of glass are attracted by the same quality of refraction that they enjoy when they look at faceted jewel stones. From earliest times in Alexandria, glass was made to imitate jewels and to delight the eye with its dazzling quality. Perhaps for this very reason Chinese glass did not reach the heights of popularity in America attained by European or American glass. Jade in all its shades from mutton-fat white to the most intense jade green was the first concern of Chinese glassmakers. Their glass also imitated lapis lazuli, turquoise, coral, agate, jasper, malachite, and sardonyx, stones that have an opaque quality and are translucent only to a degree—when the surface is highly polished or when they are cut extremely thin.

Since these natural stones were found in abundance in China and were carved for the upper classes (into beads and pendants especially), there was just no demand for glass. Certainly the workers and peasants would hardly be interested in vessels that could not withstand heat or, if broken, could not be repaired. Therefore China was rather late, historically speaking, in producing glass in any quantity, and the Chinese do not give themselves credit for perfecting glassmaking, perhaps because they considered it of such minor importance.

The *Wei Lou,* a Chinese historical work based on the records of the Three Kingdoms of the period A.D. 221–264, enumerates ten colors of opaque glass (*liu-li*) imported from the Roman Empire. However, there is reason to believe that glassmaking probably began much earlier in China, for discovered in the tombs in Loyang (dating back to the Han dynasty at the latest, and believed by some experts to date back to 400 B.C.) were glass beads that contain barium, a substance not known to occur in Western or Near Eastern glass before the nineteenth century.

In addition to the beads, several other pieces of glass made in the same forms as Chinese jade tomb objects, including a pi, a cicada, and a fish-shaped girdle pendant, were found in the same tombs. These are of greenish or bluish color, and are now decayed and brittle. The glass evidently was used as a cheap substitute for jade.

Perhaps it could be conjectured with some degree of confidence that from very early times glassmaking on a limited scale produced beads and decorations for various purposes. But the glass referred to in the Later Han dynasty is known to have been imported in ingots and carved in the same manner as stones. And as early as the T'ang dynasty (618–907) it is recorded that the artist Wu Tao-tzǔ is supposed to have originated painting inside glass bottles or vases.

We are often asked how the Chinese painted inside an already molded bottle or vase, and especially inside tiny lamp finials and snuff bottles. It is an exceedingly tedious process. The object is first treated with magnetic oxide of iron ($Fe_3 O_4$), which, mixed with water, forms a coating suitable for receiving paints. A sketch is made on the outside of the bottle, and then the artist lies on his back holding the bottle to the light. With a fine-tipped brush bent at a right angle, he follows the outside line that he sees through the bottle, beginning at the bottom and progressing to the opening, until the painting is completed.

In the year 1680 a glass factory was finally established in the palace at Peking. It is known that the productions of the atelier were called "kuan liao," or imperial glass. All varieties of work were represented, including monochrome pieces, pieces made of layers of different colors superimposed and subsequently carved, and pieces either of clear or opaque white material decorated with painted designs in translucent enamels. The director of the imperial factory, Hu, using the sobriquet "Ku Yüeh Hsüan" (Ancient Moon Terrace), was famous for his work in glass during the reign of Ch'ien-lung (1736–1795). Some of his pieces were sent down to Ching-tê-chên to be reproduced by Tang Ying, the director of the porcelain industry, because the emperor considered porcelain a nobler medium than glass.

Tang Ying was so impressed with Hu's work that he began to use Fang Ku-yüeh Hsüan, which means "Copy of the Ancient Moon Terrace," on his porcelain reproductions. This has caused some confusion to collectors of both glass and porcelain, but in China if a piece of work is above reproach, others try to imitate it; and they show their admiration by using the originator's name in one form or another on their own pieces.

Peking glass vases and bowls, particularly the white, which may be enameled like porcelain, were made to look so much like porcelain that only the trained eye can distinguish one from the other. Hu was most famous, however, for his snuff bottles and other articles so perfect that they were indistinguishable from carved stone.

There is no doubt that by using pure minerals for color and barium for brilliance, the Chinese were able to produce glass of unusual beauty despite their seeming carelessness in allowing bubbles and clay to remain in the finished products. The wide range of shades in green and turquoise were made by adding copper to the pulverized mixture; antimony accounts for the beautiful yellows, arsenic for the white; amethyst resulted from adding manganese, and the early pinks were made by the use of gold, but it was soon found that copper, through a deoxidizing process, could be used to make a wide range from red to pink.

Glass snuff bottles available today are of several types:

1. Opaque glass intended to simulate stones. Imperial yellow is the favorite, but other colors are also highly desirable: rose pink, turquoise blue, jade green, jade white, and a bright tomato red; also varieties with swirls in them to simulate wood as well as stone.
2. Overlay glass in contrasting colors. These are either carved or just very carefully overlaid in cameo fashion in designs on the surface of the bottle.
3. Bottles painted inside, with or without overlay borders. The overlay is usually in bright red, blue, green, or yellow.
4. The Ku-yüeh Hsüan type, enameled like porcelain, is extremely rare.
5. Those glass bottles carved in the Hu method to look like jade, agate, carnelian, lapis lazuli, and other stones.

Very few of these bottles are available with matching saucers. Now and then a saucer or a cup is sold that really belongs with a snuff bottle, but a complete set is rare.

Recently, new inside-painted bottles have been appearing. The knowledgeable collector will recognize them immediately. The painting is of poor quality and the colors gaudy. This new opaque glass is too smooth, though the glass is of good quality. Upon examination with a magnifier, one should see wear and patina on antique glass, and tiny pits, and even in the best of the old glass there are minute granules of clay.

Paperweights were made in China and a few were exported. They are rare, but the glass quality and colors are recognizable. They were made with many of the same techniques as were used in the making of Western paperweights.

This chapter would not be complete without mentioning a few other items of Peking glass (in addition to the beads discussed in the next chapter) that are favored among collectors. The charming pots of glass flowers, the frames of glass flowers, China lily bowls, cigarette sets, pin boxes, even salts, as well as vegetables, fruits, animals, and birds, all were made for export.

Since Europe exported glass flowers at about the same time (1920s) as China, it is necessary to watch for the purely Chinese characteristics. The leaves of the large and better-made type are thick and cut, not molded. They are an intense green, but not transparent. The flowers can be either transparent or opaque glass, but the petals are not obviously molded. They will have a ' sharp cut look, a "dripped

163. Glass flowers set in teakwood frame; ca. 1920.

164. Glass flowers set in teakwood frame; ca. 1920.

165. Freestanding glass flowers, tomato red with vibrant green leaves; ca. 1920.

wax" finish, or a crepe-paper twist. The larger flowers are attached to the stems with the wire encircling each petal where it meets the center of the flower; framed flowers usually have the stem molded into the glass. In the prunus type there is a hole in each petal through which the wire is inserted. The stems are made of iron wire (often rusty) twisted with silk wrapping, and the trunk is covered with a kind of rubbery papier-mâché material. The stamens are of thin wire (sometimes coiled), and have tiny colored beads at the ends. Some of the stamens have been finished with little globs of glass.

The frames are clearly marked "China" on the back, and the bowls too have "China" scratched on the bottom, but since the flowers frequently have been removed from their frames or pots and are all "scrunched up," it is necessary for the collector to recognize them without a label. They can easily be cleaned, the stems rearranged, and the plant restored to its original beauty.

In addition to small objects there are large carved fruit bowls, also huge vases that simulate wood; and there are two-layered pieces cut to expose the white underlayer and create geometrical patterns. Cobalt blue bowls with etched Chinese characters are prized by collectors. In addition, there are large fluted plates in semitransparent glass (an obvious attempt to appeal to the American market). The range of hue is wide, with the peacock blues being most common, but the collector comes to recognize the distinctive Chinese glass colors.

We recently identified a set of red purple glass dishes by noting that each bowl and plate was of a different weight. Closer inspection revealed other distinctive characteristics: ground foot rims, ground edges, and bubble and clay particles, in addition to considerable patina.

166. Always with a small electric light hidden in the center flower, this type has molded transparent yellow green leaves and is not Peking glass. Ca. 1920.

All added to the conclusion that we had found a set of Peking glass dishes, possibly of eighteenth-century manufacture.

The medicine bottles pictured in illustration 167 are quite interesting because of the techniques (as varied as the shapes) used in their production. One was molded in two sections and the seams are clearly apparent. Another seems to have been molded, and then to have had a piece of pure clear glass tubing inserted while the glass was in a plastic condition. One of the most fascinating was molded but has a blown inner core. The square one on the necklace shown in the next chapter is an example. (*See* illustration 170B.) The flat-flask pill bottle appears also to be a blown-mold type. All those shown are sheered and ground on the top and have a slightly green cast; therefore, although they may be of relatively recent manufacture (possibly the 1930s), they were made by techniques developed long ago.

Finally—two forms of painting on glass are interesting for the

167. These are patent medicine bottles, although now persistently called "opium bottles."

collector to seek. The most available are the lantern paintings (illustration 208). These were made by coating one side of plain glass with a mixture of magnetic iron oxide and water and painting the picture on the coating. As on the inner-painted snuff bottles, this coating lets the painting show through to the other side, and when the glass is put in the lantern, the light heightens the color quality and beauty of the painting. These panels are not very expensive. Much artwork of this kind was commercial, designed for export to be used in restaurants in the United States. However, some lantern panels are quite charming and make good wall hangings or table screens.

Mirror paintings were popular in Europe during the chinoiserie period (1660–1790). Europeans sent their own mirrors to China to be decorated, since they felt that Chinese glass and the Chinese method of making mirrors were unsatisfactory. The artist painted the picture from the reverse side of the glass; that is, he scraped away the mercury coating as he painted his picture. It was necessary for him to visualize each stroke as it would look from the front of the mirror, and in order to achieve proper perspective, he also had to paint the picture in reverse.

In other words, instead of painting the background first, as is usual, he had to paint the details of the foreground figures first and gradually fill in the background as he finished the picture. The artwork in these is competent but stilted; the colors, however, are very bright and clear. Mirror paintings are, unfortunately, far more expensive than the quality of the art justifies, though they are certainly spectacular collectors' items. We have noticed a few that seem not to have been painted on a mirror, but directly onto glass in oil paints, with the outer edges of the painting surrounded with opaque black or blue paint, thus achieving a mirrorlike appearance.

For those who enjoy searching for the unusual, there are lampshades with copper frames that enclose paintings on silk sandwiched between two layers of spun-glass rods. The rods, which are no thicker than a toothpick, are placed very close together so that they make a corrugated surface. The two layers are put together in opposite directions, at a slant. These ingenious little pieces are indeed treasures.

It would probably be impossible to name and describe the many items that were and are called Peking glass, but it should be pointed out here that most of the glass actually came from Poshan in Shantung Province. There were also many factories in or near Canton, and so it is certainly acceptable to refer to the glass as "Chinese glass."

168. Lampshade made of two layers of spun-glass rods with watercolor paintings in between. The layers are placed at an angle, on the bias, and the effect is that of a piece of embroidered fabric.

9

BEADS, BANGLES, AND BAUBLES

IN AND AROUND POSHAN IN THE NORTHERN PROVINCE OF SHANTUNG, the largest producer of glass in the nation, women sat with their children and made glass ornaments. Families went to the glass manufactory and bought pulverized material or glass rods for making beads. It is reported that the hills of Poshan looked as though they were on fire because of the hundreds of "backyard furnaces" that burned day and night to melt the glass. We know this was happening in 1850; we believe it was also taking place long before that time, perhaps during the Ming dynasty or earlier.

One man who remembers watching his aunts at work in South China not far from Canton (for glass beads were made in many locations throughout China) told us that long bamboo reeds were dipped into troughs of wet clay slip, then taken out and dried. When the reeds were ready—and it is assumed that large piles of them were prepared in advance—two people would hold one reed as a third poured threads of molten glass at intervals on it. The two end people twirled the reed, making the glass form into beads. When the glass had hardened but not yet cooled, the reed was laid on a bed of dry clay. When completely cool, the beads were shaken off into water to be washed. This method accounts for the large amount of clay in the core of the old lantern or tassel beads; it also accounts for the bubbles that add interest and beauty to Chinese beads and certainly help in identifying them.

These beads come in two main shapes, spherical and elliptical, and in all sizes. The larger beads were strung, 100 to a strand, on heavy hemp cord and taken to the glass contractor, where the workers were paid and then bought another quota of glass to work with. The fact that beadmaking was individual work and that the variation in color combinations was extremely wide makes the Chinese bead an exciting exploration in color alone.

It is difficult to pinpoint when these beads first arrived in the Americas. We know that trade between China and Portugal, Spain, the Netherlands, and England began very early, and it is quite possible that beads were transported to Europe before Columbus's time. Though it is not our purpose to trace and account for the final destination of glass from the Orient, our research leads us to a rather firm conclusion that the "padre" and/or "pony" beads that the American Indian accepted for trade in the southwest United States and Mexico were indeed made in China. These were a simple mandrel-wound bead (one made by twirling a ribbon of molten glass on a rod until it cools and hardens).

History reveals that before the end of the sixteenth century Manila had become the Spanish equivalent of Portuguese Macao. Chinese and other Eastern traders brought goods to Manila, which were redistributed from there. Trade across the Pacific to the New World was limited to one city—Acapulco, on the Pacific coast of Mexico. It received a regular, though restricted, amount of wares from China, Japan, and the East Indies, including raw silk, satins of all colors, velvets, gold and silver brocades, cushions, carpets, musk, ivory, writing boxes, beads, precious stones, and porcelain. Therefore, although there is some controversy regarding the origin of the Southwestern Indian beads, there is every reason to believe that they came to the New World from China via Manila.

However, the beads reasonably easy to purchase today, and still beautiful though they are of a later date, came here between 1850 and 1940. They were used to decorate lampshades, as lamp pulls, window-shade pulls, tiebacks for draperies, and for the corners of card-table covers (these covers were weighted down at the corners by huge spheres of glass or disks called "pancakes" by Americans). Available too is a wide assortment of circlets from finger rings to extra-large bracelets (found on baskets, evening and knitting bags), as well as double gourds (also used for lampshade pulls), large and small teardrops with enameled brass fittings or brass fittings decorated with kingfisher feathers.

Many collectible beads and circlets have been removed from sewing baskets. Tiny beads were also used on shoes and purses and other

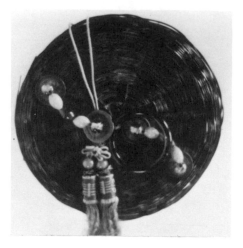

169. Basket with glass beads
and ring.

items calling for bead decoration. Buying a lantern to get the beads (which the distaff side of this writing team has been accused of doing) can prove rather expensive, but nevertheless many of the most unusual types were on lanterns. Portieres, too ragged to use, are a wonderful source of unique Chinese beads. Not to be omitted are the long strands for the flappers of the 1920s.

All these beads are now much in demand by people interested in the hobby of macramé or string knotting, since they have large holes and their colors greatly enhance the macramé. Even the tiny beads usually have a hole large enough for regular two-ply twine. The chopped or clear glass bugle bead used on portieres can be placed at appropriate spacing on macramé belts, and glass circlets of various sizes enhance the work of both crocheting and macramé.

Collectors love Chinese "melon beads." These were made in sapphire blue, amethyst, clear crystal, and delicate pink, all transparent glass. They are irregular and actually look like little melons. Those originating in Europe are very evenly made with the sections tent-shaped instead of rounded.

The Chinese are known to have imitated the Venetian styles—that is, to have used inlays of copper filings and overlays of tendrils and roses. (Often a plain yellow or white bead was completely overlaid with red.) No matter how ornate the bead is, the clay core shows in a Chinese bead, and small amounts of clay and telltale bubbles sometimes disrupt the flow of tendrils or cause a flaw to appear through the overlay.

The use of copper filings to make goldstone we know is of Italian invention. Chinese goldstone beads are made by the technique of twirling on the mandrel. They have very carefree bands of gold, or sometimes the whole bead will be swirled with gold. Venetian-style goldstone beads are perfect and usually made with inclusions in a specific design deep in the glass.

The eagerly sought carved glass bead is still another collector's delight. Most of these are from China and are an intense sapphire and/or cobalt blue. It can only be assumed that the color limitation of carved glass beads is attributable to the fact that natural stones such as amethyst, rose quartz, clear crystal, and carnelian were readily available for carving into beads. The carving on stone or glass usually consists of a longevity symbol or just a series of grooves placed at right angles on the surface of the entire bead.

Square or rectangular beads with beveled edges on beautifully knotted strands are not too difficult to find and not really expensive. Faceted beads were made in China, but are of rather poor quality— the facets are molded rather than cut. Even the quality of the glass is quite poor.

After one has collected enough beads for a necklace or two, it is a challenge to find a lamp finial that is painted inside. These came from China and were used on lamps made from Chinese vases. Lamp finials make very elegant necklace pendants!

The mandarin necklace is also available. It too has carved beads, some even pierced like jade carvings. These necklaces are rare and rather expensive.

How can you be sure a bead is Chinese? With experience, the colors become familiar to the seasoned collector, but if the color is questionable, then the traces of clay, the air bubbles, and the ever-present irregularities in the bead contour make identification comparatively easy. A word of caution is necessary for the purist. Fine-quality beads were made immediately prior to World War II in China and Hong Kong. These are relatively free of clay, but close examination will reveal irregularities in size, bubbles, slight swirls, and large holes. At that same time Czechoslovakia exported beautiful beads that looked quite oriental. The original strands were often knotted between the beads, as the oriental beads were, but the Czech beads are more likely to be in graduated sizes and of higher quality glass, and the holes are small. East Indian and Pakistani beads have black-tar cores.

Glass jewelry was made in China just prior to the invasion by Japan in 1937. It is of very good quality; the clasps are good and, though old, have not tarnished. The manufacturers made small glass ornaments to simulate jade, and they do indeed look like good jade. Carnelian, amethyst, lapis, and coral were also imitated. Their resemblance to the true stone is very convincing and can fool the amateur. These pieces are stamped "China" in one place or another on the metal findings. On

170A. Peking glass bead necklaces. *Left to right:* (1) Goldstone with pink elliptical beads and cloisonné pendant. (2) Chartreuse and turquoise clear glass beads with square medicine bottle. (3) Heavy, deep blue porcelaneous beads with enamel pendant. (4) Varicolored beads with enamel lantern piece. (5) Imitation jade beads, circlet, and pendant.

170B. Carved bone, wood, and seed necklaces. *Left to right:* (1) Carved wooden beads, three ojime beads, and a pendant of water-plant seed and a carved peach pit. (2 & 3) Carved bone beads interspersed with reconstituted amber beads. (4) Carved peach pits; the pendant is a single large peach pit carved with a complete village scene.

necklaces, the clasp may be marked "Made in China" or "Made in Japan," or any other country for that matter, though the beads may not be from that country. People have a habit, when restringing beads, of using any clasp they have on hand. However, there is a rule of thumb that can be at least an indicator: The Chinese most often used a large, simple spring-ring type of clasp. On their best beads they used a screw type. They also used a shuttle type, usually on small chokers of natural stone.

The Japanese made exquisite bronze beads inlaid with gold and silver or engraved with beautiful designs. These were spaced on chains, and many different shapes were included on one chain—cylinders, spheres, ellipses, and cones, all very tiny, usually on choker-length strands. We cannot recall ever having seen these as general export trade jewelry, so we must assume that they were originally sold only in Japan. Very small, well-carved bronze roses on chains are more available than the other type, but are expensive.

Japan exported large quantities of flat metal plaques in the form of flowers and butterflies, enameled with black and decorated with gold. These were spaced on a good chain with a screw-type clasp. They are being manufactured again, but the later ones are larger and more showy than the old ones.

Carved beads of all types were made by the Japanese—coral, ivory, shell, and wood. They have a distinctive Japanese design, and the workmanship is impeccable.

High-quality glass was and is produced in Japan, and of course Japanese beads are unsurpassed for originality and perfection. Simulated pearls were exported by the ton from Japan before and immediately following World War II. These were made by dipping lovely grayish white beads in a liquid pearl essence. Collectors find it fun to soak these beads for a few minutes in hot water—the pearl coating peels off easily and the gray white beads underneath make beautiful filler or spacer beads.

For the most part, the Japanese used two types of fasteners. One, a flat mounting decorated with a piece of glass to match the beads, was closed by inserting a spring made of a simple bent piece of metal. The other type of fastener was adjustable, the same sort of arrangement used on much of today's costume jewelry; at one end of the strand was a simple, rather large hook, which was hooked over a five-inch bead-and-chain extension on the other end of the necklace. Many of these necklaces were made in tiers of from three to five strands, each graduated in size. The glass is of high quality. These are not antique and are not distinguishable from American and European beads of the same period. Their charming shapes and the combination of deep blue, orange, orange red, beige, brown, and black coloring are their main differentiating feature. Japanese beads may also have inclusions of strips of gold or silver foil.

Japan manufactured heavy brass necklaces and bracelets, which were decorated with seed and melon-shaped glass beads of many varieties: swirled, striped, molded, overlaid, foil-imbedded, and so forth. A necklace made up of these beads (removed from the brass) can be exceptionally interesting and beautiful.

The most prized Japanese beads, however, are the large white porcelain variety decorated in underglaze blue or a combination of the blue, rust red, or black and brown. These were used for drapery pulls, lamp pulls and finials, and scroll weights. They may be round or shaped like large pecans.

Among strictly Chinese baubles of the past are those decorated with kingfisher feathers. (*See* color section; also illustration 171.) These brilliant, iridescent, turquoise blue feathers were used on the costume jewelry of the highest-ranking women in China. Though the decorative pieces meticulously accented with these feathers must be considered only artcraft, they are exquisite and the collector cannot but be entranced by their beauty. Hair ornaments spun of silver or gold and decorated with kingfisher feathers and pearls are rare, but they can be found. The feathers adorned all types of pins and eardrops, headdresses of every conceivable type, and most fascinating of all—fingernail protectors! A small brooch made brilliant with these feathers can be bought today for about the same amount as a well-made piece of modern costume jewelry—$15 to $20. The most exotic pieces have moving parts attached to minute springs, and they dance in the light. A favorite is the sectioned fish, which is usually attached to a pin or bracelet.

Brass bracelets, necklaces, and brooches inset with many uniform pieces of coral, turquoise, and lapis lazuli were intricately made. The metalwork is good. (The products emanating from Hong Kong since the Korean War are not comparable.)

The charm bracelet made of silver filigree and enameled is an appealing bauble that fascinates the lover of things made in another era. The charms may be miniature Chinese lanterns with all the decorations in metallic enamel, or rickshas, jointed fish, a pleasure boat, a bride's sedan chair, even an abacus with movable counters.

Filigree has been made in many parts of the world, but each area has its distinctive designs. Naturalistic flowers, butterflies and other insects, and spiders are favorite Chinese subjects. The silver or gold thread (or a combination, such as a silver spider web with a gold spider) is fine but does tarnish. A bath in liquid silver polish will restore any piece to its original beauty.

Small carved lacquer plaques were put in ring and pin settings. These are available in cinnabar red or in a soft green. The plaque used for a large brooch may have an entire Chinese scene carved on it. Carved lacquer beads are scarce now and rather expensive.

Carved shell and carved ivory, though being produced today, were finer at an earlier time, the carving much more intricate. Both shell and ivory take on mellowness with age. Items made prior to 1940 were set into metal frames into which the clasp was molded. The newer variety have a clasp glued directly to the shell or ivory.

Cloisonné beads are especially prized; they were most often used on the ends of the drawstrings on embroidered evening bags or as finials on old lamps. Japanese cloisonné beads were used on inros or on ladies' hairpins. Both are rather expensive, starting at about $10 each. We have seen only a few pairs of cloisonné earrings, but recently found two exquisite spheres with one hole; they were on hairpins at one time.

Today there is a great demand for the beads carved from seeds, wood, and bamboo. Someday we would like to own one of the peach-stone boats depicting the Sung dynasty poet Su Tung-pu sailing in a pleasure boat with his famous poem of over three hundred characters incised on the underside of the vessel. Recently we bought a peach stone carved with a beautifully detailed scene including pine trees, Chinese people, birds, and houses. We have also found cuff links, half a pit being used for each link. Perhaps we shall have to be satisfied.

Miniature Buddhas are much sought after, carved from seeds, ivory, or boxwood. The Chinese carved them to put on chain necklaces. The new ones now being imported seem to be made of plastic or synthetic wood may be pressed or carved.

Sandalwood beads are popular too, and if they have been kept in a container, they will still have their fragrance though they may be many years old.

We are sometimes asked about a bead that looks like a miniature dried-up prune. It is made of rose petals or dried medicinal herbs, which have been crushed, mixed with a glutinous vegetable material, then dried. These beads make very good spacers and are always a source of comment. Perfumed paste roses (made from a colored thick rice paste, molded, and dried until very hard) strung into a

171. A tiara of brilliant turquoise blue kingfisher feathers and pearls over silver. It was worn on important occasions—with or without the bird (phoenix) hairpin—by a Chinese lady of rank. The hairpin, made from two tones of kingfisher feathers on silver, could be worn separately on informal occasions. Notice the coiffure of the lady in illustration 58.

necklace or rosary were favorites with American women in the 1920s. They are collectible items today and quite easily available.

Simulated or reconstituted amber—that is, amber made from boiled, strained, and dried resin or from laminated bits of amber—shows up in many forms: carved or faceted, clear yellow to deep cherry red. These beads are very beautiful, and to most people are indistinguishable from genuine amber. It would be misleading to try to help the amateur collector by giving the rules for detecting "real" amber. However, if a strand of beads made up of carved wood, carved bone, and a few dried herb beads is enhanced with a few simulated amber beads, the collector should not scorn the necklace. But to pay a high price for a necklace of purportedly antique amber beads is risky unless they have been appraised by an expert.

As a finale, here is an experience we had while bead hunting. We were looking for Chinese glass beads simulating the jade called "moss in the snow," which is white with just a spot or two of bright green. We had asked at many places and had pawed through countless trays of beads. Finally one dealer answered, "Yes, I have two here under the counter. You know, I can't leave beads out on top anymore."

We looked at them in disappointment. In the dim light they appeared to be cracked, and we felt that a dollar apiece was a little high. At length she offered to let us have them for 80 cents and we took them, still thinking we had paid too much for just a couple of baubles. At home, when we examined them carefully in a good light, we discovered we had two jade beads worth at least $10 each.

And so what is glass to one person may be jade to another!

LACQUER

LACQUER, LIKE SILK, IS ANOTHER PRODUCT THAT HAS BEEN IN USE since time immemorial. Chuang Tzŭ (ca. 300 B.C.), an exponent of the Taoist philosophy, preaching his doctrine of uselessness, offered the lacquer tree as an example, saying that it invites damage to its body because it produces lacquer.* From Chuang Tzŭ's statement, we know that lacquer was in wide use in his time and perhaps much earlier. Traces of it have been found on buried bronzes and pottery tomb figurines dating before his time.

By the Han dynasty (206 B.C.–A.D. 220) lacquer was used not only as a preservative but also for decorative purposes. Recent excavations have unearthed Han dynasty baskets and toilet boxes expertly decorated with lacquer of several colors. Perhaps the most striking specimen is a basket uncovered in a tomb in northern Korea, where the Han Chinese established the border province of Loyang. The decoration shows groups of people seemingly engaged in spirited conversation. This is not only an example of superb lacquerwork, but also one of the few existing examples of early Chinese figure painting.

As later developments showed, the versatile material lent itself

---

* Lacquer, a sap from the sumac *Rhus verniciflua,* or lacquer tree, is poisonous and can cause severe allergic reactions in some people. Those who have lived in the Orient may have seen people with their faces swollen to twice the normal size and their eyes mere slits, victims of lacquer poisoning. The discomfort is severe, and recovery takes about two weeks. A mere whiff of the fumes can start the allergic reaction.

to a great variety of uses, and many ingenious techniques were developed. Buddhist statues of the T'ang dynasty (618–907) were often made of dry lacquer; many of them are still in existence today. The unique sculptural work was done by applying many coats of lacquer, reinforced with fine fiber or cloth, over a clay, papier-mâché, or wooden form, which was withdrawn when the lacquer dried. Such a statue not only shows texture and translucence approximating living flesh, but its weight is considerably reduced for easy carrying in processions.

Lacquer, when applied on furniture, woodwork, and cabinets, gives the finished product not only a coat of lasting toughness, but one of elegance and dazzling beauty. It is easy to understand the amazement of Westerners when they first visited the Orient. One compared the Chinese house to such "a gigantic mirror that a person can see his face reflected wherever he looks." Another praised the Chinese table as being "so smooth that any spilled grease can be easily wiped off and therefore no tablecloth is ever needed."

When a lacquerer decorates, he paints with an almost unlimited palette of colors: white, turquoise blue, yellow, green, aubergine, black, red, brown, silver, and gold. However, he is tempted to be lavish with gold, silver, and even mother-of-pearl inlays, and thus his work tends to be on the rich and ornate side, as can be noted on the screens, cabinets, and commodes that are popular in the West.

172. Chinese tea box —black lacquer with gold painting; ca. 1880.

173. Japanese tray inlaid with ivory and mother-of-pearl on red lacquer ground; ca. 1880.

174. Japanese tray showing street scene, perhaps of the Edo period, has polychrome lacquer and gold of three different shades; ca. 1900.

During the early part of the T'ang dynasty (618–907) the Japanese sent students and craftsmen to China, and the art of lacquering was probably one of the techniques they brought back to Japan. But they gradually discarded stylized designs of Chinese origin in favor of naturalistic pictures, which were characterized by gaiety, freedom, and the constant use of new techniques and means of expression. From the Kamakura (1185–1333) down to the Edo (Tokugawa) period (1600–1868), which is best known to Western collectors for its lacquer inro, or medicine boxes, so many styles were created that even mere enumeration is impossible in a short chapter like this. Certainly nothing can compare with the elegance of Japanese gold-sprinkled black lacquerwork, with or without inlays of mother-of-pearl, tortoiseshell, ivory, or metal.

Because of the climate in Japan, which is particularly suitable for lacquerwork, the Japanese were able to turn out more finished and beautiful products. And during the fifteenth century, the Chinese sent craftsmen to learn the Japanese techniques of applying lacquer. Lacquerwares were in fact the most popular household items in Japan. It has been theorized that their love of lacquer delayed their porcelain making until the sixteenth century.

The Koreans may have used lacquer even earlier than the Japanese. Unfortunately, because of the small quantity produced, Korean lacquers were hardly noticed by Westerners except for a few specimens brought back by Western connoisseurs and missionaries. Their lacquer products, however, display extremely good taste, retaining an archaic flavor reminiscent of the Chinese T'ang period, with pearl and sometimes tortoiseshell inlay. This inlay work, done by a painstaking technique known as "lac burgautée" in the West, is a popular type of decoration on lacquer objects, and the Chinese, the Japanese, and the Koreans are extremely good at using the technique. Mother-of-pearl, tortoiseshell, and animal horn are used. We might mention here that the Koreans have a special product called painted horn (Hwagak). The hard shell-like part of the animal horn is scraped until transparent and then cut and flattened. Designs are painted on it, and the painted side glued to the lacquered object. Done this way, the design will not wear off.

As has already been mentioned, almost no export was made of Korean lacquerwork, and because of the frequent foreign invasions, which devastated the land, very few early works exist today. During the Korean War (1950), Americans left a great quantity of empty cannon shells. The thrifty Koreans reclaimed them and turned them into beautiful lacquer vases with exquisite inlaid mother-of-pearl floral designs. A few of these were exported, but many were brought home by returning veterans. Now they have become collector's items.

During the last three centuries Chinese and Japanese export lacquer goods have enjoyed great popularity. Large lacquer panels or screens were often cut up and made into chests, commodes, and cabinets by Western cabinetmakers. However, there are two classes of products that are uniquely Chinese: (1) furniture and screens decorated with incised, chiseled, and/or built-up lacquer designs, often inlaid with mother-of-pearl, ivory, and semiprecious stones to form human figures, architectural features, and scenery. These products are popu-

175. American cannon shell of Korean War vintage with Korean lacquerwork. Chrysanthemum design of mother-of-pearl is inlaid on black lacquer. This vase, which weighs over four pounds, was probably made from a five-pound shell after the removal of fuse and powder.

176. Large Chinese covered box for sweetmeats; diameter 18″. Incised lacquer is of the Coromandel type. Ca. 1880.

177. Three of a set of five Chinese lacquer trays, Coromandel type. Ca. 1900.

larly known as Coromandel, a name derived from the Indian seaport town of Coromandel, whence they were exported to the West; (2) carved lacquer objects such as vases, boxes, plates, and sometimes even tables and chairs. Both these categories are in low relief and present a different effect from the painted lacquer.

Coromandel work was done by applying a coat of a gray claylike substance over a soft wood base, which was first covered by cheesecloth to hold the clay in place and to prevent it from cracking. Then the elaborate designs were incised or carved or applied in relief on it. Finally, several coats of decorative lacquer of various colors were painted over it. Beautiful screens and furniture made in this fashion can last for centuries if they are placed properly—that is, in a location without excessive dryness or humidity, and never in direct sunshine.

As soon as dampness or overdryness causes the clay to crack, bulge, or peel, it is difficult to stop it from falling apart. However, there is one drastic procedure to try: Fill in the damaged area with a good filler and touch up the surface with paint that matches the original colors. When this is dry, cover the repaired area with a coat of clear plastic paint, using the kind that produces a high gloss. Rub this down with fine steel wool until it matches the whole object in glossiness. If the object is in bad shape, it is sometimes necessary to cover it all over with two or three coats of the plastic paint. This treatment is equal to wrapping up the article in an airtight plastic sheet that will prevent further deterioration. (*See* Chapter 15.)

A good screen represents the investment of a large sum of money, and it is also expensive to have one repaired. The buyer should examine such a piece carefully before purchase—go over every inch of it in a good light. Slight damage along the edges is acceptable, but should be repaired as soon as possible. On the other hand, if the central part of any of the panels has cracked or warped, that means the lacquer or the lacquer-clay combination has separated from the wooden base. Avoid any such screen like the plague!

Carved lacquer is often known in this country as cinnabar. Actually, "cinnabar" merely means the red-color type. It is also made in brown, plum, green, white, black, or combinations of two or more colors. To call every piece of carved lacquer "cinnabar" is like calling every dog a Pekinese.

To make carved lacquer, a number of coats of lacquer, sometimes fifty or more for a fine specimen, must be applied on a thin wood or metal base until a thickness suitable for carving has been built up. This is then carved to a depth of usually from $\frac{1}{8}$ to $\frac{1}{4}$ inch, into a landscape

178. Chinese plate of wood, with gold lacquered design of five dragons in relief; diameter 12″. Ca. 1900.

179. Chinese plate of carved brown lacquer made on a copper base; diameter 9½″. Marked Ch'ien-lung, but probably ca. 1900.

or a floral or some other design. Sometimes lacquer of several different colors was applied in successive layers. On such pieces, when the carver desired a certain color—for instance, green—for the trees in a landscape, he would cut to the green layer and expose it on the overall pattern.

During recent years, up to the 1940s, imitations of carved lacquer were made using a sticky putty-like substance, which could easily be pressed in a mold. This kind of material never really dries; it can be as messy as chewing gum, particularly when the piece becomes old and the protective coating wears off or melts in very hot weather. Quite often when a person has bought one of these imitations, it is solicitously wrapped in a piece of newspaper by the dealer who lacks experience with Chinese antiques. The new owner puts his find in the trunk of his car and speeds home to show his family the beautiful vase he has bought. When he proudly unwraps his treasure before the inquisitive

180. Chinese carved lacquer box in cinnabar red. Base is wood.

181. Chinese carved lacquer box in white. The knife carving makes the design stand out sharply. Ca. 1920.

182. Chinese lacquer box in white; ca. 1920.

eyes of his family, the old newspaper has become an integral part of his carved lacquer vase. There is no way to separate the two except by delicate surgery—with a sharp razor blade.

Even authentic carved lacquer can suffer heat damage. We can bear witness to an incident of that kind. In the midst of an absorbing conversation, a guest absentmindedly placed her hot coffee cup on her hostess's heirloom carved-lacquer plate, which had been specifically brought out to show her. To her horror, she could no longer lift the cup without also lifting the lacquer plate! This type of misfortune happens all too frequently. Most noncollectors cannot be expected to know that antiques are different from ordinary household items. In other words, a lacquer plate to them is a plate, and should function as one. (Indeed, a a guest in our own home used an 1840 gold and black lacquer pin tray for an ashtray.) It is the owner's duty to protect his treasures from being abused.

For another example, there was the collector who graciously brought from a trunk an antique Ming rug to show a visiting friend, who had arrived accompanied by a large family and two dogs. After the rug had been duly admired, the head of the visiting family said, "Now, kids, all of you walk over the rug so that you can tell your friends back home you have walked on a ten-thousand-dollar Ming rug." Before the shocked host could protest, the five kids, led by the father, all in tennis shoes full of dust and car grease, and two German Shepherds made a procession over the 400-year-old rare rug!

Imitations of Chinese carved lacquer are also produced in America. The material is some sort of plaster, and the pieces are reproduced in molds made from genuine Chinese carved lacquer objects. Then they are painted over with appropriate colors. These imitations are much

183. Chinese black lacquer trays with mother-of-pearl inlay; ca. 1920.

184. Black lacquer vases (Chinese) decorated with silvery lacquer; wood bases. Ca. 1920.

heavier than the genuine pieces. The white plaster shows wherever there is the slightest chip or damage.

Carved pieces, no matter how well finished, always show some sharp knife marks. It is very easy to tell the authentic from the imitation, of either the putty type or the plaster type. The difference is as transparent as that between cut glass and pressed glass.

185. Tabletop decorated with inlaid mother-of-pearl on black lacquer bears a scene of "Four Old Men on Mount Shang." The word "Shang" is in the vulgarized version. This could mean that the Chinese artisans did not know the correct version, or that the table was made by Japanese or Korean workmen who did not know Chinese well. Any of the three oriental countries could have produced this specimen, which measures 31″ x 44″.

IVORY AND ITS SUBSTITUTES

THERE IS AN OLD SAYING IN CHINA: "IVORY DOESN'T GROW IN A DOG'S mouth," which is often used as an effective put-down for anyone who prattles nonsense.

People in the Orient value ivory—elephant ivory, that is. Therefore we shall exclude all the other materials that share the name ivory: walrus ivory, hippopotamus ivory, whale ivory—and canine ivory, if there is such a thing.

It is believed that in ancient times elephants roamed the wild expanse of central China, and that each autumn kings and princes staged safaris to hunt this big game. Many archaic ritual bronze pieces were cast in the likeness of elephants or decorated with elephant-head handles. The ancient Chinese also valued the tusks, which were fashioned into tools, utensils, and decorative items. When these large animals became extinct in China, perhaps because of changing climatic conditions, the fossilized tusks and bones of prehistoric animals were used as substitutes, but these substitutes are easily distinguished.

Genuine elephant ivory shows a unique mellowness and a smooth soft texture. It has often been likened to the skin of an oriental beauty. If we examine a piece of ivory, we can see that it has a zigzag pattern of lines in a cross section, but lengthwise the lines appear almost parallel. Old ivory often splits along these lines. Although ivory darkens with age, it never loses its beauty or soft luster.

Bone, a popular but cheap substitute for ivory, shows no lines,

186. This rhinoceros shows the split lines of old ivory. Ca. 1880.

and is homogeneous in structure. A close examination will prove that it has many small holes or channels, which are the natural conduits for providing nourishment for the growth of the bone. In color, bone is chalky, and when it is old it develops an unpleasant dry and yellow look; the tiny holes collect dirt and dust, which are difficult to remove.

The tusks of prehistoric animals, which were sometimes used for carving extra-large specimens, have a dull look and are valued less than elephant ivory. Walrus tusk is small and has a brown, granular core that must be cleverly utilized or hidden in carving. This drawback limits its usefulness to the making of small items.

During the fifteenth century, the court of the Ming dynasty sent seagoing vessels to Southeast Asia and Africa searching for exotic animals, particularly the "ch'i-lin," a mythical creature supposed to symbolize the virtues of an enlightened monarch. They brought back the giraffe, which was believed to be akin to the ch'i-lin, and presented it to the emperor, who was greatly pleased. They also brought back ample supplies of ivory, thus giving the art of ivory carving a new impetus. Many figurines of that era still survive. And some carvers, both Chinese and Japanese, even today still dutifully put the reign mark of Ch'êng-hua (1465–1487) under the base of their finished pieces and have the objects smoked and soaked in strong tea to give them the Ming look. It may be appropriate here to repeat an important warning for beginning collectors: Reign marks on oriental antiques should not always be taken seriously.

During the last hundred years, great quantities of ivory work were produced: models of palaces and pagodas, figurines from an inch to two feet high, incense burners, vases, animals, birds, insects feeding on a head of cabbage, and so on. Some were touched up and enhanced with pigments; others were left in the natural color, depending on the carving tradition of the locality where the work was done. And, of course, we must not leave out snuff bottles! They usually bring three or four times more money than other items of the same amount of work and material. After all, who knows the story that such a small bottle might tell?

Perhaps an elegant little dark brown specimen once belonged to the Dowager Empress's favorite eunuch, who even as he daintily measured out the fragrant snuff with the little spoon attached to the lid was secretly plotting to dethrone the reigning emperor. If the imagination is given free rein, that little bottle can indeed look sinister and brimful of oriental intrigue.

Antiques with exotic and often fictitious background stories capture the popular imagination. Consider the tale associated with the blue willow pattern. Westerners designed the pattern, and the Chinese collaborated by manufacturing not only the dishes but also a tear-jerking oriental love story for the hostess to narrate over roast beef and mashed potatoes. We ourselves have been made captive listeners to it on countless occasions. Worse yet, we are always asked to confirm the story; and like well-mannered guests, we do so, albeit unwillingly.

In the case of ivory, the so-called "doctor's dolls" are a good example. These dolls portray a voluptuous reclining female figure in the nude, about six inches long. As the story goes, the doctors in the Chinese royal household were forbidden to examine female patients. When the queen or a princess was indisposed, the practice was for the doctor to bring along a "doctor's doll," one of these nude female figures (in Chinese eyes, an utterly indecent article), and hand it through a thick curtain that concealed the royal patient. (A recent antique show had one specimen that measured at least twenty inches—it would no doubt require a husky doctor to carry it on his back to his patients!) The patient would hand the doll back through the curtain, to the doctor, with the royal finger pointing at the place where the pain or ailment was located. Well, that is a good story, all right. But can anyone imagine a palace physician daring to bring such a thing to a royal patient? He'd be beheaded before he was through with his diagnosis!

A sexless diagram of the human anatomy carved or incised on an ivory plaque was no doubt once used by the physicians. However, the "doctor's doll" is one of those objects of erotica that belong in the same category as the ivory clamshell with either a three-dimensional carving of a man and woman in an erotic position or (for much less money) a painting of the same in a real shell. These were sold to swaggering playboys and young apprentices in the big city or to foreign sailors on

187. The so-called "doctor's doll." It would be unthinkable for any Chinese doctor, let alone a palace physician, to bring such a titillating nude figure to his female patient for her to point out the location of her ailment.

leave in Shanghai. But thanks to the exotic yarn, a "doctor's doll" sells at present for about $150, whereas a piece of carving of a different design requiring the same amount of material and work sells for about $50.

A dealer we know recently bought several dozen new copies of the doll, and he complained that even the wholesale price was $55 each. His dolls came from India. The workmanship is good. The only difference is that the Indian figurine has a tall double hair knot, and is decorated with both upper and lower arm bracelets; otherwise it is a very faithful copy of the Chinese model.

Both the Chinese and Japanese are expert carvers of ivory and there is really no necessity to trace the origin of a beautiful piece. However, we will deal with the differences briefly. The Chinese adhere to traditional themes—Taoist immortals, the God of Longevity, Kwan Yin (the Buddhist Goddess of Mercy), and the legendary beauties. The Chinese figurines are slender, graceful, and fully clothed or robed. The

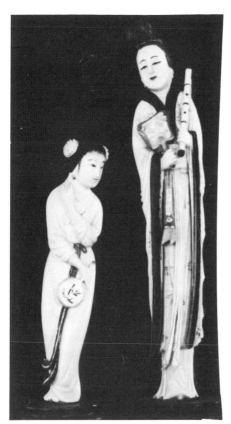

188. An aristocratic lady (9″); and her maid (6″); ca. late nineteenth century.

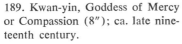

189. Kwan-yin, Goddess of Mercy or Compassion (8″); ca. late nineteenth century.

Japanese figures are likely to be more naturalistic: geishas playing musical instruments, fishermen with their catch, and so forth. The Japanese also like to stress the virility of their male figures—the men always show strong leg muscles and are slightly bald. They are more adept too at antiquing their work with lacquer.

A unique class of Japanese ivory work deserves special mention: the netsuke. There are two ways of pronouncing the word—net-ski, or ne-tsu-ke—and there has always been argument as to which is the correct way. Once we took the matter up with a Japanese lady, the wife of the proprietor of an antique shop.

190. Carved card box with cross design in the center; ca. nineteenth century.

191. Netsuke, both carved ivory. The round type is often called a manju. *Dr. and Mrs. Marvin Hockabout Collection*

She was very happy to pronounce it several times for us, and we distinctly heard her say "ne-tsu-ke."

While we were talking, her husband, a retired American navy man who had married the charming lady while he was stationed in Japan, came into the store from the back room, and wanted to know what all the discussion was about.

"It should be pronounced 'netski!' The 'u' has no sound," he said. "Right, Iris?" He looked at her for confirmation.

"Yes, you are right. It's 'netski,'" she readily agreed, as a good oriental wife should.

So there the matter stands. The Random House Unabridged Dictionary lists both pronunciations as being correct. Perhaps even lexicographers, in their quest for enlightenment, could have run into the same type of situation as we have.

A netsuke is a toggle that is part of the inro, or medicine box or pouch, a Japanese carried on his belt. The custom of wearing these boxes is supposed to have begun during the early seventeenth century.

192. Japanese medicine box or box for small personal items (inro), with netsuke (the toggle to keep the box fastened to the sash), and ojime (bead to keep the sectional box closed.) *Dr. and Mrs. Marvin Hockabout Collection*

The function of the netsuke was to keep the box from falling off the belt. Gradually it developed into a decorative item, and carvers competed with each other to produce netsukes of the most ingenious designs and superb workmanship. Anyone who occasionally visits antique shops is familiar with and perhaps enchanted by such popular designs as a baby chick emerging from a broken shell (and you can be sure that is not the only ivory baby chick emerging from the shell in the antique stores in your town), or those representing the masks used in Japanese Noh drama, or the numerous traditional gods, or even caricatures of Europeans. Some have movable heads or eyes, a feature that does not necessarily contribute to their artistic value.

Many netsukes are carved from walrus ivory, wood, or staghorn, and these are just as valuable because here it is the workmanship that counts most. Some are signed, others not. However, it is often difficult to track down the name of the individual carver. Of course, like other antiques, a netsuke must be worn or handled for many generations to acquire a beautiful and smooth luster.

In Tokyo today there are master carvers who will make exact copies of any netsuke exhibited in the museums of Japan. You can order them through a catalogue for about $200 each, and can expect delivery in eight weeks or so after you send payment. These are masterfully done, comparable in every way to the originals. All you need to do is carry the netsuke in your pocket, fondle it in your spare moments, and watch it attain the patina of the old pieces.

A great quantity of the netsukes on the market today are of synthetic material, so the beginning collector should be cautious about buying hastily.

During the past half-century many imitation ivory objects have been made of celluloid, wax, or plastic material, and some of these even

193 A & B. Although the Chinese are preoccupied with the idea that the delicate ivory is an appropriate medium for only the ethereal and the graceful, the Japanese use it to interpret the realistic, the broadly humorous, even the grotesque. This carved ivory father and son (shown in both front and rear view) are obviously having a good time catching frogs or insects—no generation gap here. Ca. 1850.

show the distinctive parallel lines of the grain pattern of real ivory. In the past few years reproductions of Chinese ivory figurines, made by European manufacturers, have flooded the market. They are as heavy as genuine ivory pieces and have good color. But on imitation pieces the seam marks from the molds can generally be detected. Genuine ivory, being hand carved, always bears some knife marks that can be seen with a magnifying glass; so the collector should never be without a magnifier when hunting ivory pieces. Some of the best imitations are carved out of chunks of heavy synthetic material; therefore buyers should not only look for the grain pattern of genuine ivory but also use the needle test explained below.

Once an avid but indiscriminate collector of ivory showed us his large collection. Unfortunately, many of his pieces were made of synthetic material of one kind or another, though he had paid good prices for them. The dealers who sold them to him were probably not dishonest—they really knew no better. During our conversation, the subject of distinguishing genuine ivory from imitation material came up, and we tactfully suggested a simple test. The next time we visited him, he had discarded one fifth of his collection.

The test is very easy, and anyone can make use of it unhesitatingly. Take a small needle and heat it until the tip is red hot. Then stick it immediately into the base of the item. If the needle goes in as much as ⅛ inch with ease, the material certainly cannot be ivory or bone, for in either of those materials the needle will leave only a pinprick or a tiny burned mark. Do not test with a lighted match, as some cheap imitations might go up in flames.

There is a great difference in value between items carved from ivory and from bone—not that all things made of bone are necessarily second rate, particularly when bone serves the purpose better. For instance, mah-jong tiles are almost always made from bone. Some ivory sets were no doubt made, but they are fit only for the ladies' boudoir where the game is played with feminine gentleness. When men sit down to play—and usually a game lasts well beyond twenty-four hours—they bang the tiles vigorously on the hardwood table to keep themselves

194. Group of female figurines in semi-archaic costumes; Chinese, ca. 1900.

awake. Ivory tiles would surely split along the grain lines, and so here bone is a more suitable material because it is tougher and harder.

For the same reason, decorative beads with intricate, thread-thin openwork are usually made of bone. In this type of work the difference of the material will not show, and the difference in the value of the raw material is negligible because the amount used is small. Bone, however, stands the wear much better than ivory.

195. Embroidered fan with carved ivory frame; Chinese, ca. 1900.

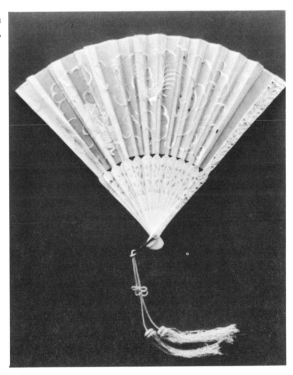

WOOD–FURNITURE AND CARVINGS

A RETIRED MISSIONARY SHOWED US THE PIECES OF ANTIQUE CHINESE furniture she had acquired in China during the early 1900s. They were made of huang hua li, a type of wood that was popular for furniture making during the Ming and Ch'ing dynasties but increasingly scarce the last hundred years. There was beauty and strength in the simple lines of her furniture. The workmanship was so good that, even though no nails were used, no piece showed a sign of ever having been repaired, reassembled, or glued in more than three hundred years—for that must have been the true age of her collection.

We asked her why her rare antique furniture was in the front room. She passed her hand repeatedly over one of the satin-smooth, amber-colored surfaces as she answered, "I never worry about it. I leave it here for people to sit on just like my American furniture. But you know, whoever sits on one of these straight-back chairs for five minutes will have to stand up or change chairs. I think"—she smiled— "the reason why these Chinese chairs last so many ages is because they're so uncomfortable."

Indeed, Chinese furniture of the formal type was not made for comfort, but for etiquette so that the visitor would be constantly reminded to sit straight. It was also designed to add dignity to the already imposing and austere main hall. This was particularly true in northern and central China where the influence of officialdom was strong. In southern China, away from the court, elaborate carving and

196. Teakwood chair; ca. 1850. The Chinese prefer this type of simple, strong structure.

197. Teakwood stool of simple and sturdy design, ca. 1850.

mother-of-pearl inlays were often employed to relieve the severity of the dark, heavy hardwood. The most extreme decoration appeared on the export items, with scaly dragons winding over every inch of a chair or the legs of tables, which were often topped by rose-colored marble.* They are chinoiserie of the worst type.

But not everything with dragon motifs is necessarily Chinese. The Japanese, whose taste is also for the simple and austere, exported a great quantity of this chinoiserie furniture to the Western world. It was either cheap and massive, made of soft wood stained very dark to simu-

---

* In northern and central China, Ta Li marble from Yunnan, a white stone with black markings that resemble rockery or simple landscape paintings, is preferred for tabletops and chair backs.

late hardwood and carved with sharp knife cuts; or made of hardwood with good rounded carving, well polished, and beautifully lacquered in rosewood or mahogany color. The expensive items often have the signature of the maker carved on a piece of ivory or bone and attached to the leg or lower part.

Naturally Japanese chinoiserie furniture is often mistaken for Chinese. Recently a flamboyant dealer displayed a cabinet at a big antique show. Before the show opened, there had been a tremendous amount of publicity in all the local newspapers. The cabinet was mentioned as a rare antique Chinese piece priced at $15,000. The picture in the newspaper, however, was a little fuzzy, as newspaper pictures can be. We had serious misgivings about the identification given the cabinet, and so decided to have a look at it.

Upon arrival, we saw the dealer surrounded by a large worshipful audience listening to his lecture about the treasure: "The last Chinese emperor ruled for only three years," he said. (*True.*) "This magnificent cabinet with the imperial dragon on the front was especially made for him." (*False.* The last Son of Heaven had enough subjects pursuing the trade of cabinetmaking so that he had no need for furniture "made in Japan.")

The cabinet, an elaborately carved and ornate piece, was most certainly of Japanese make. For one thing, part of the construction at the top was lathework. The Chinese do not use this technique in making cabinets. For another, the carving made lavish use of straight stalks of Japanese iris, and iris and wisteria are favorite Japanese motifs. Finally, the "imperial dragon" had only three claws or toes. If it had been made for the emperor of China, it would have had five.

It might be useful here to elaborate a little more on the "toe-counting" procedure. There are two types of dragons: the archaic dragon, which looks like a salamander, and the modern dragon with a scaly body, horns and whiskers on its head, and always showing its sharp claws. Theoretically, the dragon with five claws was reserved for the royal house, the four-toed for noble families and high-ranking officials, and the three-toed for ordinary people. This tradition began during the Ming dynasty. In practice, however, the tradition was not always observed. The five-toed dragon was a royal prerogative that could not be usurped. Very old lacquer or cloisonné pieces decorated with the imperial dragon motif sometimes have had one claw on each foot chiseled out. This was done because, during the time of the monarchy, people were afraid of being severely punished for possessing things that should be found only in the royal household. But for the sake of prestige, who wouldn't want a four-clawed dragon? And who couldn't

198. Two panels, probably from cabinets, carved with Chinese scenes and lacquered in red and gold; ca. 1850.

find somewhere in his family tree an ancestor with an official rank? Also, the Chinese have a deep traditional respect for the dead, and so in ancestral portraits (popular collector's items in the West), the deceased, regardless of his social position, was accorded the honor of wearing a four-clawed dragon robe. Hence, in later ages, the three-toed dragon was as good as forgotten. Immediately after the overthrow of the Ch'ing dynasty in 1912, every Chinese, if he wanted to, could live royally, using five-clawed dragon furniture, eating from dishes decorated with five-clawed dragons, and wearing five-clawed dragon robes!

On the other hand, the Japanese traditionally used the three-toed pattern. Therefore, a porcelain vase, or a cabinet for that matter, with a

199. These panels, probably also taken from cabinets, are carved in deep relief and lacquered red and gold; ca. 1875.

three-toed dragon can be either early Ming, pre-Ming, or of Japanese make, although when the Japanese copied a Chinese piece they would use a four-clawed or five-clawed dragon now and again.

So a five-clawed dragon on a chair or robe or cabinet may mean only that the article was made after the downfall of the last monarchy in 1912 and has nothing to do with anything imperial. In fact, a four-toed dragon item may be much older and therefore more valuable. However, we must again stress that all rules have exceptions and none is necessarily foolproof. In making any general statement about the fields of art and antiques, one always has the "out on a limb" feeling.

200. Threefold table screen of light-colored teakwood with inlaid boxwood decoration; ca. 1850.

201. Top of an oblong teakwood table; ca. 1880. Such elaborate carving is too ornate for the Chinese taste.

To Westerners, all Chinese, Japanese, and Korean furniture is teakwood. Actually, teak is a light-colored wood chiefly found in India. But since this is not a book on botanical terminology, it is not the best place to try to correct misnomers that have persisted for two or three hundred years. One of the large importers of Chinese furniture in San Francisco cannily classifies his stock (composed of all types of hardwood) into three categories: light-colored teak, medium-colored teak, and dark-colored teak. We think his practice has merit.

The Chinese use several kinds of dark-colored hardwood for furniture making, but their favorite is a type of rosewood they call "redwood," which is certainly not the California sequoia! Another favorite is tsu tan, or red sandalwood. These woods are close grained and need no filler and often no lacquer. The best Chinese furniture is polished with water mixed with the finest powder made from unglazed pottery roof tiles, then finished by hand rubbing until a uniform satin sheen is produced. Sometimes walnut, oak, and Chinese cedar are used as cheap substitutes. They are coarse and porous, and need both filler and lacquer to give them a smooth and nonporous surface.

Teak curio stands, including stands for vases and vessels of every description, miniature tables, table screens, and mirror frames carved in dignified simplicity or delightful virtuosity have artistic value of their own. Collectors cannot resist them purely for their own beauty and not only as accessories. Large screens incorporating porcelain plaques were made of dark teak to provide contrast, as were the finest picture frames. Lantern frames were usually of dark teak to set off the paintings on either glass or silk. The heavily gilded and fancifully painted lanterns produced in southern China, however, were made from camphorwood, a lightweight wood. These were sometimes made so large that weight became an important factor to consider.

Camphor is a most useful wood. Every collector of oriental antiques must own one or more camphor chests, be it a full-sized one or a six-inch miniature. (A collector specializing in Japanese antiques would no doubt prefer a Tansu chest, often made of a native wood called kiriwood, which not only shows ingenious workmanship but also can be displayed as a handsome piece of furniture in a Western home.) Some are carved in low relief with traditional scenes. The most expensive camphorwood types are embellished with expertly carved, inlaid plaques of boxwood.

Camphor, other kinds of soft wood, and occasionally teak were carved to decorate temples, restaurants, and other public buildings. There was no limit to the designs and patterns: scenery, folk heroes,

202. Teakwood tray inlaid with mother-of-pearl; ca. 1880.

203. Teakwood boxes, approximately 11″ x 6″, inlaid with mother-of-pearl in elaborate landscape designs; ca. 1880.

▶

206. Close-up of the lantern panel shown in 205. The clothing is cut from brocade and pasted on; the faces are made from paper-thin sheets of ivory.

204. Wood plaque with the characters "t'ai-chi" (the ultimate limit) in the center, and the eight trigrams (considered to be the oldest form of Chinese written characters); lacquered in red and gold. This type of Taoist plaque is believed to have the magical power to ward off evil spirits.

205. Lantern with teakwood frame and painted silk panels; ca. 1850.

▶

207. Close-up of another panel from the lantern in 205, which has four different scenes.

208. Lantern with teakwood frame and painted glass panels; ca. 1900.

209. Front of camphor chest inlaid with boxwood panels; ca. 1900.

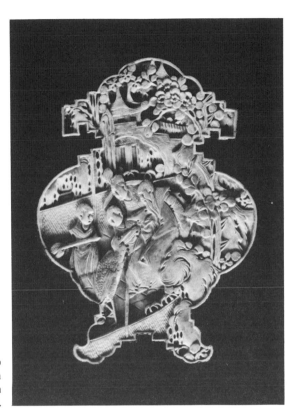

210. One of the top panels of the chest in 209, showing the design carved in the boxwood.

Taoist immortals, traditional symbols, and naturalistic motifs. Sometimes a layer of flowers and birds would be superimposed on a background of coins, swastikas, or bats and pierced through to reveal a mirror. A carved life-sized pine tree or blossoming prunus with magpies and peacocks perching on it would serve as a room divider. Chinese joss houses (temples) and restaurants built in the late 1800s or early 1900s in this country were decorated with a profusion of these woodcarvings. They were usually lacquered with a brown undercoat, then a coat of cinnabar red; the highlights were painted in gold.

Many of the old Chinese buildings in the United States are being torn down, and these large carved pieces and related odds and ends are eagerly sought by dealers and collectors. Often the gold paint has either tarnished or partly worn off, and people try to touch it up with dime-store gold paint, which is thick and dull and cannot match the oriental gold. It is better to be satisfied with whatever original finish is left. The

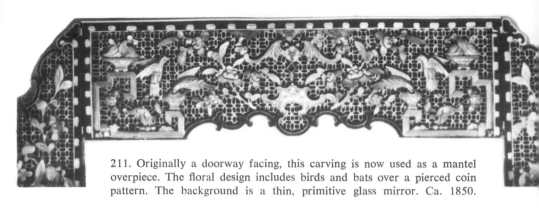

211. Originally a doorway facing, this carving is now used as a mantel overpiece. The floral design includes birds and bats over a pierced coin pattern. The background is a thin, primitive glass mirror. Ca. 1850.

212. Taoist immortal crossing the sea is carved wood lacquered in red and gold—a small piece broken from decorative woodwork.

traditional Chinese method of renewing tarnished gold paint is to crush a clove of garlic and rub the juice over the paint. In our opinion no benefit results, and we therefore do not recommend the practice.

Boxwood has long been used for small items such as combs or miniature carved panels and to make contrasting inlays in dark wood. Boxwood is a very slow-growing tree. The texture of the wood is so fine that small figurines carved from it rival old ivory in beauty and are sometimes mistaken for ivory.

213. Pair of red and gold bookends is carved with wood ducks under a canopy of lotus flowers and leaves. Ca. 1900.

Although the Japanese are credited with the invention of the folding fan, the Chinese and Koreans as well considered the fan an essential accessory for ladies and gentlemen of culture. Fan ribs were carved beautifully of the best material—ivory, bamboo, or wood; and the fan itself was made of strong laminated paper and silk to withstand constant folding and unfolding. One side was decorated by an eminent artist and the other by a noted calligrapher. In the old days, a gentleman would own several dozen fans and use a different one every day, for fans were prestige items in the Orient. In summer, those of sandalwood were preferred because the wood has a delightful fragrance.

Bamboo, a versatile material, was (and is) widely used to make every conceivable useful and decorative item. Its pliability makes it suitable for baskets, and those used in the oriental household were done with great ingenuity and artistry, and beautifully lacquered. Hanging scrolls made of narrow bamboo sticks laced together had flowers, birds, and landscapes stitched in, to look much like embroidery work. Other bamboo items are brush holders, brush handles, and the armrests popular with scholars and artists. Objects carved from gnarled bamboo roots are greatly treasured.

Rattan baskets and boxes are beautifully woven and seem never to wear out. Rattan, woven on a bamboo framework, has long been a favorite material for informal furniture such as lounge chairs. Such furniture is lightweight, and easy to carry around, and because of its low price has always been very popular. Anyone who has used a rattan chair will gladly testify to the fact that the oriental people do have some comfortable furniture after all!

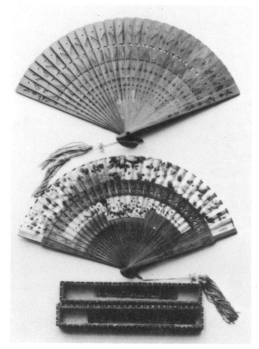

214. Carved sandalwood fans with glass cases; ca. 1945.

215. Carved bamboo sections (height 14″) of this type are common in oriental homes for holding various household articles. Japanese.

13

TEXTILES—EMBROIDERY, BROCADES, RUGS

WE HELD IN OUR HANDS A WEDDING GIFT—A PICTURE, ONE OF MOUN-tains and mists with a lone rider on a donkey making his way along a precipitous pathway toward his home. Was it embroidery or painting? Only by close examination could we discern that the delicately painted mountains and clouds were overlaid with fine threads of embroidery, giving the picture the look of a pencil sketch.

This was a gift we would treasure because it came from a cousin. The time was just after World War II, and the authors were in Wusih, near Shanghai, where Mr. Chu grew up. Wusih is famous for many things, among them Ku hsiu, a type of embroidery that may be the finest in the world.

Mr. Chu's cousin was the principal of the city's only embroidery school, which had been started by their aunt, in her time the leading feminist of the town. The school had opened during the last gasping days of the corrupt Manchu dynasty. Her pioneering effort to teach young ladies the art of embroidery along with academic subjects in a Western-type school caused many a raised eyebrow among the town's important people.

At the time of our visit, this cousin was nearing the age of forty, too old for working as an embroiderer, as the art demands perfect eyesight. Her nineteen-year-old niece and pupil had become the best artist in the school and in the entire district, for that matter. It was she who had painted and embroidered our wedding gift.

216. Embroidery, Ku hsiu type, done by a cousin of the authors. It is often mistaken for a brush painting.

217. One of two panels embroidered in the "hundred son" theme. (The Chinese like to have many sons—up to 100.) This panel has fifty boys playing games in several groups. Ca. 1880.

We returned to America with samples of the work done at the school in Wusih. Though we gave away many pieces as gifts, it is fortunate that we kept several for our own collection.

The Ku hsiu method of embroidery is so called because it was perfected during the Ming dynasty by the family of Ku in Shanghai. It was always recognized as the superior type, for the process made it possible for the worker to create exquisitely realistic pictures of flowers, birds, insects, and butterflies. Even fine portraits were embroidered by skillful artists. Large frames covered with pure silk satin were arranged on turntable pedestals, and the subject to be embroidered was penciled in very lightly. The embroiderer used tufts of floss dyed in a wide range of hues, and needles so fine that one could use them only if the fingers were soft and without calluses. The shading that made this embroidery so special was the result of using the embroidery floss like a paintbrush, overlapping a stroke here and there, changing shade or color at will. The front and reverse sides are almost indistinguishable because the embroiderer carefully covered the ends where different colors were introduced. Knotting was not necessary.

Very little of this exceptionally fine work is available today because it could not withstand the wear on clothing. Embroidered scrolls that were hung in the light have faded and begun to disintegrate.

Embroidery on gauze, which may have been used in a lantern (inset between two layers of glass) or attached on top of a bright-colored silk satin to give an elusive quality to the background of the entire piece, was also produced. It is not often found in good enough condition today to be of any satisfaction to the collector.

Massive amounts of a more durable type of embroidery work produced in Peking, Canton, and Hunan were exported to Europe as early as the sixteenth and seventeenth centuries, and later to America. All the known embroidery stitches were used: satin stitch, long and short stitch, stem stitch, Peking stitch or French knot, drawnwork, basket weave, couching and laidwork, and many others. The cutwork done on linens rivaled that of Milan or Madeira.

Embroidery for mandarin garments for the Chinese was largely done in Peking. This brings to mind the "forbidden stitch" we are so often confronted with. From its literal translation, Americans have assumed a false grandeur for a term that actually means nothing more than "something made in the Imperial City or the Forbidden City in Peking." In no way should it be construed as indicating that the highly skilled knotted embroidery work was forbidden to other people. It was just that this work was first done by the imperial embroiderers on imperial garments.

218. Part of a lady's mandarin robe; ca. 1880.

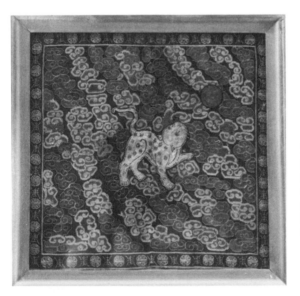

219. Part of a man's long mandarin gown. In the center among the clouds is a celestial animal. The stitching in gold and silver thread is in low relief over blue gauze ground. Ca. 1900.

Canton factories produced most of the export work. In Hunan Province were made great yardages of embroidered work for draperies, bedspreads, and pillow cases. Known in China as "Hsiang hsiu," these were made primarily for the domestic market, but were also exported.

220. Pillow case embroidered with very bright and intense colors; Hunan type.

K'o ssu and Chinese Tapestry

K'o ssu, or silk tapestry work, was never produced for export and very little is available in this country, but if the collector knows what to look for, it can be found. At a charity-sponsored flea market just a few weeks before this writing we discovered, tucked under several other fabric pieces, a very exciting K'o ssu tapestry. It is the front of an imperial garment. The price was fantastically low; had it been framed and offered in an antique shop, the price would have been six or eight times as much. Recently a set of four large (8″ x 30″) K'o ssu pictures of ordinary workmanship was sold at an auction for more than $75 each. One dealer at a flea market priced a simple repeat design of K'o ssu in absolutely threadbare condition and only one yard long at $30.

This type of weaving (for it cannot be considered embroidery) was evidently executed in two or three distinct ways. There is confusion among investigators and even in the Chinese writings as to how it was actually done. The background of the material was obviously woven with fine thread (both warp and weft were silk); then tiny shuttles were used to open up the background at the predrawn outlines of the design, which was then woven into the openings. This assured a smooth change from background to figure, and it accounts for the narrow space around the design, which makes it look as if the background had been cut and a reweaving process used to fill in the open place. The appearance accounts for the name K'o ssu, which means "cut silk."

When one examines this tapestry work carefully, he cannot help being impressed with the exquisite results, the flat surface, the sameness of either side. The material is very thin and was used principally for summer garments. One mandarin coat took a year to make; therefore even the nobles prized such garments highly.

Heavy tapestries were also made by the Chinese, and these were sought by the Europeans, especially after the Chinese had learned to follow European taste in designs. The Chinese did much finer work—23/24 warp threads per centimeter and up to 116 weft threads on a centimeter of warp, whereas the best Paris tapestry shows 8/11 warp threads and only 22 weft threads per centimeter. In China only silk was used for the warp and weft, and the weavers took much care in preparing their own threads—spinning and dyeing them themselves. One of the unique features of all Chinese tapestry, as well as of the embroidery, is that the gold threads they used did not tarnish. It is still not fully understood why. Some Ming dynasty tapestries have gold threads that still retain their luster today.

Brocades and Other Silks

Dear to the heart of the Westerner are the silk brocades of old China. Garments and yardage of these are still available, many in good condition because people just could not bring themselves to wear out clothes made of such lovely material. In the late nineteen-thirties, Chinese manufacturers began to mix rayon thread with the silk to make a cheaper and more durable fabric, but these brocades are recognizable because of their coarser texture.

In and near Hangchow brocade pictures were—and are still—made. These show scenes of the beautiful West Lake, famous as a resort area, and pictures of important personages in what are really woven portraits. Recently a TV news clip showed portraits being made of Mao Tse-tung in the identical way and probably on the same machines that produced portraits of Chiang Kai-shek and Franklin D. Roosevelt in the early 1940s.

After modern methods of printing textiles were introduced to China, large quantities of printed silk were exported to the United States. But they were made into American-style dresses, and it would be difficult to identify an old silk garment as having been made from Chinese silk rather than from silk produced in other countries such as Japan or France.

Trousers and coats of lacquered silk are unique summer wear, and the collector will enjoy having one of these garments to add to his collection. They are made of a small-figured brown brocade that has had an application of black lacquer to give it a shiny surface finish and also to make it slightly stiff so that it stands away from the body, thus making it relatively cool for summer wear.

Raw silk, meaning the coarse and less desirable silk, dyed and printed, as well as pongee, has always had favorable reception among Americans. Both are available today, so they are not collector material unless made up into an item of special interest.

For the collector, embroidery is probably of the greatest interest among textiles. It is commanding unrealistically high prices. Even inferior work exported in the late 1930s is priced too high. Many small table pieces are of this coarse workmanship. However, if a piece from a mandarin garment is in reasonably good condition, even though faded, it can be salvaged by cleaning with a high-quality solvent, then mounted and framed. It is even possible to touch up the color with a textile paint.

Entire mandarin garments, if in good condition, are well worth a price of up to $200. If, however, they are falling apart, it seems fool-

221. Hanging scroll; ca. 1930. The design is embroidered on a screen made of thread-thin bamboo sticks.

ish to pay more than a few dollars for them because the buyer will not be able to restore them.

We have had many compliments on a restoration job we did with a huge, elaborately embroidered and decorated silk that had hung for fifty to seventy years in a Tong meeting room in San Francisco. After lifting out the gold dragons and ch'i-lin of laidwork from the borders by careful use of a razor blade, we retouched them with gold paint and applied a final coat of very thin, clear plastic varnish. They make handsome wall hangings. The main picture of a huge phoenix was carefully mounted on a piece of Pellon (inner lining material) and framed. The tiny mirrors were left intact but refinished with gold around the edges, and now they dance when the light reflects from them. It is, of course, not hung where exposed to direct sunlight because the silk would continue to fade and disintegrate.

222. Embroidered handbag with Peking glass handles; ca. 1900.

Other embroidered items of interest are handbags (these are often mounted and put in frames), vanity sets that include a fan, coin, and cosmetic bag, and other small pieces. Often the work is excellent and because the owner has treasured a piece, both sides are in good condition and it can be mounted and framed, or the whole set can be so treated. These were often part of a trousseau, to be presented as gifts to the bride's new relatives.

Rugs

Rugs should be hung on the wall! This is literally true of the early Chinese rugs. The collector hangs his rugs if he hopes to protect them them from the wear of hard-soled shoes. To be sure, such rugs do last a long, long time, but with steady daily use they will become worn at the edges and wherever they are constantly walked on. Today's collector of small but very beautiful samples of Chinese rugs will want to use them as wall hangings or chair covers.

The Chinese rugs available now rarely belong to the "antique" category (meaning 100 years old or more). To begin with, those older than 100 years, if they have been used as floor covering, no longer have great beauty. Such old rugs are usually faded and worn almost beyond recognition and are of doubtful value. (Those of great value are just not available to the ordinary collector.)

The Chinese seem to have lost the art of their earliest type of rug-making—i.e., felting. In the museum at Nara, Japan, there are examples of this eighth-century work. Japan also has in her possession many Ming rugs.

Rugs made throughout the Ch'ing dynasty for the royal palace were used for generations, and when the Manchus left and the palace was ransacked, they were taken by the plunderers. Now, about the only antique rugs that are available to collectors are those made since 1850 and sold on the open market. The rugs of that period were made in the far northwestern region of China by quite primitive methods. They were made as covers for the "kang," or heated brick beds, to be slept on at night, or to place over the doorways of the nomads' homes. Many were made for saddle blankets. Few of these rugs ever came through to the port of Tientsin until after 1850, at which time Tientsin merchants began to buy and contract for them and to export a few.

After the establishment (1912) of the Republic of China and the expansion of trade with the West, merchants began to demand more and more rugs for export. So rugmakers set up factories (usually of one or two looms) and proceeded to have the workmen weave rugs according to specifications. At first these were of poor quality because the variation in the wools and the dyes was so great. There was an attempt prior to World War I to use aniline dyes, which German manufacturers were exporting. These first chemical dyes were not stable; the colors ran and caused the rug to look spotty after it was washed. (It had to be washed after weaving to further cleanse the wool and to shape the rug.) After washing, the rugs were hand dyed (painted with a brush) where the color had run. Now and then a collector will come across one of these.

When aniline dyes were perfected, the Chinese rugs made for export became a truly fine item. The colors used at first were reproductions of the old vegetable colors used during the Ming dynasty. But by the 1930s the manufacturers had expanded the color range to appeal to the Western market. Rugs produced during those years are really worth buying. Although they are not as durable as the rugs of India or the Near East, they have a beauty and charm of their own. The Chinese never tried to compete in the number of knots per foot. The early rugs were made completely of silk, but later (after 1850) both the warp and the weft threads were cotton and the knots wool. Sheep's wool was and is the most desirable material for the pile of the rugs; but camel, yak, and other animal hair was used, often mixed in one rug.

Perhaps one of the most fascinating things about Chinese fabrics is the use of various emblems and symbols as a means of decoration. Rug weavers first followed the bronze designs, then the designs of the potter,

223. Blue and white rug in the Ming style; ca. 1850. (Real Ming rugs are very rare.)

224. Rug, 3' x 6', in Po-ku (hundred antiques) style. Although it is obviously well worn, the colors used and the condition of the dyes indicate it is no older than 1900. The center vase of forced plum blossoms for the New Year adds interest to the motifs. Center background of medium blue is surrounded by a brown sculptured frame. Border is dark blue; the "antiques" are in green, rose, blue, and brown.

225. The center part of a superb, 6' x 9', deep-pile Peking rug in rich rose with a blue border. Such stylized designs are for the Western market. Though there is some streaking and fading, the rug probably was made around 1925.

and when they began making rugs for general use in China and for export, more designs were needed and even Buddhist and Taoist religious symbols and figures were employed for decorations.

For the Chinese taste, the literati rug using symbols of the scholar —scrolls, inkstones, brush-washers, and so on—was very popular. Those with symbolic plants, flowers, and insects were also in demand, and of course the repetition of the formal Ming styles continued. The "hundred antiques" rug design found favor with all lovers of Chinese culture. These designs were composed of many, not necessarily a hundred, treasures such as vases, tripods, screens, and so on.

The technique of carving or sculpturing (cutting around the design to make it look raised) enhances the appearance of a rug, but it requires rugs with a deep pile. The early attempts at this art were frequently disastrous because where the pile was cut the knots were loosened, and the rug came apart rather soon after it was put on the floor and used.

Rugs from Paotow, which are often small and round, were treasured because of their great compactness of texture (some almost like thick felt) and because they are really a picture in weaving. They are indeed rugs for the wall.

Japanese and Korean Textiles

Japan was introduced to the processes of silk making, embroidery and brocading, and printing through China. When brocade making was mastered, the nobles demanded the material for their own garments.

The "patchwork" effect came about in Japan as a result of one nobleman's demanding that all the pieces of brocade he had in his possession, whether originating in Europe or China, be made into one garment. This became the fashion. Japanese workers adapted themselves well to reproducing the exquisite patchwork brocade in one piece. The early work was very stiff, which accounts for the fact that these gentlemen, the nobles, looked in pictures as if they had wire framework under their clothes. Later the brocades could be made either very stiff or very soft and pliable. A beautiful brocade silk or cotton obi (kimono sash) is well worth adding to any collection of oriental antiques. Of course a complete kimono would be even better.

Printed silks were first produced by the batiking method (the term coming from Malaya, its place of origin). Batiking called for making the designs in wax or a clay mixture as a repellent, then dyeing the whole cloth. When the wax or clay was removed, the design remained. At first only blue and white patterns were produced.

(The peasant cloth of inland China was also produced this way on coarsely woven cotton. The simply designed material was appreciated by all Chinese.) Later, a more intricate method of line batiking was learned and the combinations became unlimited. However, block printing soon replaced the old method, and it was no time before the Japanese had learned to print great bolts of material in short order. The first prints were copies of favorite embroidery patterns, but Japanese artists were among the first to enter the fabric-design industry. They have produced many of the world's great pieces.

From Japan also came the yards of embroidered material used for formal dresses and coats and many of the so-called Spanish shawls. These were very expensive and time-consuming to produce, and it did not take Japan long, after the introduction of the sewing machine, to adapt it for making machine embroidery.

Except for the few years during World War II when Japan ceased exporting textiles, there has been a constant flow of fabrics from that industrious country. Honest-to-goodness antique pieces would be very difficult for the amateur to differentiate. It is a fascinating field in itself.

Embroidered screens are semi-antique, and many are very handsome and not too difficult to find. For these the Japanese used a padded laidwork style of heavy, ornate embroidery usually in gold and silver thread, which, though tarnished with age, can be restored with a metal cleaner. The subject is usually an eagle perched on a precipice or flying downward to attack its prey. Now and then one can find a lily or magnolia blossom design. The frames of these export screens are of softwood with deeply cut bamboo or pine patterns.

Korea has not exported fine fabrics in the past for the simple reason that any excess she might have had went directly to Japan. Unless one has traveled in Korea and purchased fabrics there, he will probably not be able to add Korean-made materials to his collection.

Maybe a word of advice is not out of place here. The textile collector, perhaps even more than other collectors, must select his purchases with great care because they are, after all, perishable, particularly if worn or even hung on the wall, unless protected with a frame and glass. Rugs, particularly Chinese rugs of the late twenties and thirties, can be reproduced and are being copied today by the Indian weavers. Exquisite Ming-style rugs from India are coming on the market now, and when China decides to weave rugs for export the product will be superior. Therefore, one must consider carefully the worth of· a piece before being carried away with the beauty of an oriental rug.

MISCELLANEOUS COLLECTIBLES

Pewter

PEWTER HAS BEEN USED IN THE ORIENT SINCE VERY EARLY TIMES —some of the mirrors excavated from old tombs of the Chou-Han period were made of it.

The Chinese also used pewter for making altar sets—candlesticks and incense burners. The material is soft and easy to work with, and elaborate shapes and forms can be fashioned. However, because of its low melting point, a pewter candlestick can be destroyed in minutes by a collapsed candle. The heat-keeping property of pewter has made it a popular material for winepots and serving plates for hot food.

Pewter objects are often inlaid with bronze or decorated with quartz, carnelian, and glass. Similar items are being made in Hong Kong today, but the copper or bronze decorations are not inlaid; they are soldered to the surface, "appliquéd," and therefore are not flush with it.

Some beautiful old pieces have fancifully carved coconut shells fitted on the outside to act as an insulator between the hot pewter teapot, winepot, or cup and the user's hands.

The Japanese sometimes used pewter for inlays in their lacquer-work; the effect is softer and more elusive than that of silver.

Books

Books printed by the wood-block method and dating from the Sung and Ming dynasties are treasured. This is also true of the early

226. Pewter teapot has the body encased in an elaborately carved coconut shell; ca. 1850.

227. Pewter winepots; ca. 1900.

228. Yi-hsing-type red stoneware jar overlaid with pewter decorations. Made in Shangtung Province, ca. 1900.

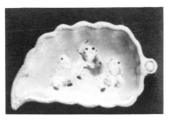

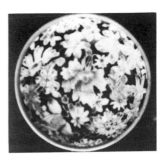

229. Small porcelain dishes encased in pewter. Many of this type, made recently in Hong Kong, are on the market now.

printed books of Korea and Japan. Hand-copied books, particularly the old ones carefully done in beautiful calligraphy, are among the highest-priced oriental antiques.

Cork Pictures

These are a special kind of art of South China. The cork material is sliced very thin, then cut and carved, and glued to a backing to build three-dimensional pictures. These are encased in a shadow-box type of frame.

230. Three-dimensional picture made of cork is a scene of Precious Stone Mountain, Hangchow. Ca. 1920.

231. Three-dimensional cork picture; 1950.

Seals

Every Chinese, Japanese, or Korean scholar or artist usually owned a number of seals executed by the best artists in the art of seal-carving. A seal could consist of the owner's name, his sobriquet, a motto, or a line of poetry. The script styles ranged from the most archaic to the modern. Seals were usually made of various kinds of stones, often fancifully carved. Those stones that show streaks or patches of blood red color (known as chicken-blood stone) are considered the choicest. Jade, ivory, metal, and wood were also used.

Ink Stick, Inkstone, and Brushes

Artists and scholars each had individual preferences amongst writing materials. Ink sticks from Anhwei were considered the best, as were brushes from Hu-chou. The most expensive inkstones were made from rocks taken from the bed of Tuan River, or from the pottery tiles of the Han dynasty. Choice inkstones are elaborately carved along the edges and at the top.

Iron Flowers

Many iron flowers show real artistic merit and are dramatic as wall decorations. There is a story about how they were invented. Once upon a time, a scholar-artist became very ill on his way to the capital and was taken care of by an ironsmith and his family. During his long convalescence, he designed many patterns for iron flowers to repay his host's kindness. After he left, the ironsmith began to make these iron flowers and sell them, and he became very rich.

Large quantities of metal flowers are now being imported from the Far East. They are machine stamped and cut in a single operation, from thin metal alloy. Then they are painted with gold or black paint or both, and fitted into standard frames. The old ones, on the other hand, are hand-wrought iron, riveted together, and are much heavier. Often they are mounted in good hardwood frames.

232. Iron flowers in teakwood frame. The flowers and leaves are heavy, hand wrought, and riveted together into one unit. Ca. 1900.

233. A recent import, these flowers are stamped and cut out of thin sheets of cheap metal.

Cut and Folded Paper

Paper folding (known by the Japanese term origami) and cutting are very old oriental arts. Devotees can create tremendously complicated patterns with just a piece of paper and a pair of scissors. Now and then a paper doll made by means of judicious folds and cuts, with papier-mâché head and body of rolled paper, can be seen in an antique store. Such items are, however, often greatly overpriced.

Puppets

Fist puppets were made and operated in China much the same as in the Western countries. Miniature stages and props were usually sold along with the puppets. Shadow puppets, however, are almost exclusively a product of the Far East. The antique type were cut from dried animal skin scraped to a transparent thinness. Each movable part of the puppet was attached to a long stick, which the operator manipulated under the floor of the stage. Like so many other items that have begun to be exported recently, these can now be bought at import stores in the United States, but the handwork is perfunctorily done.

Dolls

Oriental dolls are constructed of much the same materials as dolls elsewhere throughout the world. They range from those made of papier-mâché to elegant ones made from porcelain. There are also simple peasant dolls constructed of cloth and stuffed with straw, old newspaper, or rags. Most treasured by Americans are the opera and theatre dolls of both China and Japan. Chinese actresses have high tiaras, long ear beads, filmy dresses with elaborately embroidered panels, dancing tendrils of wire. Their feet do not show, as the doll is fastened to a pedestal. The antique dolls have actual wire and beads, hand embroidery, and brilliants made of minute glass mirrors. The modern ones are all tinselly and sequined.

The Japanese counterparts have elaborately dressed hair. The costumes and the obi, or sash, were fashioned from gorgeous satins and brocades. Many of these dolls represent Kabuki theatre characters.

Though they are fastened to a pedestal, they have the getas on their feet. The recent Japanese dolls have been cheapened by the poor quality of the material used for their costumes.

Samurai (warrior) dolls along with their ladies and their servants are a true delight for the collector.

From China come the cunning clay dolls with movable heads. When they are jostled slightly, their heads bounce as though they were nodding to the passerby. The head is attached to the body with a spring. These dolls come from just outside the city of Wusih, where they are made from clay excavated from the foot of a particular hill. All the inhabitants there, for generations, have been engaged in this craft, making every conceivable type of doll and animal from the sunbaked natural earth.

234. Chinese doll with head of painted papier-mâché; ca. 1900.

235. Japanese doll—a baby; ca. 1920.

Lately all old dolls have become very expensive, and the oriental types are no exception. For instance, a very common type of cloth-bodied doll about 8 inches tall, with a glazed papier-mâché head painted with just slightly oriental features, dressed in Chinese clothes (faded and ragged now), was priced at $59 at a recent big antique show. At the same show, a young Chinese Kuomintang officer doll with Sam Brown belt (probably one of a kind) was $250.

This brief discussion of some of the items that do not fall into the chapter categories of oriental antiques and collectibles is not complete —it could continue almost endlessly. But the varied items mentioned will perhaps provide the reader with a few clues to new collecting possibilities.

236. Japanese doll—a woman; ca. 1920.

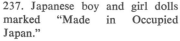

237. Japanese boy and girl dolls marked "Made in Occupied Japan."

238. Dolls representing the love story of the cowherd and the weaver, made in Wusih of sun-dried clay and colored with polychrome pigments. 1947.

239. Wusih clay dolls representing an old couple. The heads are set on springs so that they almost never stop shaking. 1947.

240. Miniature mask of a scholar, Wusih claywork, 1947.

15

CARE AND REPAIR OF
ANTIQUES

MOST COLLECTORS TAKE GREAT PRIDE IN DISPLAYING THEIR TREAS-
ures, but many unfortunately do so unwisely, with little regard for
artistic considerations and even less for the numerous obvious risks
they run. Here are a few tips that may be of help to the beginner,
though possibly they may also point to factors some experienced collectors have overlooked or ignored.

1. Display things where you can see and enjoy them—yes. But don't
   put highly valuable and fragile specimens where you must detour
   around them a dozen times a day, or where they will be a tempta-
   tation to any undisciplined visiting youngster (too many children
   today have not been brought up to keep hands off or to respect the
   difference between mine and thine), or a source of curiosity or
   hazard for badly trained visiting pets.
2. For both safety and artistic reasons, group compatible items
   together. Don't, for example, stand fragile eggshell porcelains next
   to bronzes. Put such items with "softer" things like wood carvings
   and lacquer boxes.

   Breakables like glass or porcelain can be further protected by
   securing them in position with almost invisible nylon threads or by
   fastening them to a surface with a gumlike substance available at a
   florist's or a department store. (To remove pieces fastened in this

manner, use a slow, twisting motion. Don't try to yank or jerk them free. The residue of such adhesives can be removed with cleaning fluid, but don't use them on your expensive furniture as the remover may damage the varnished surface.)

3. When teakwood stands are used in a display—and they do greatly enhance the appearance of many oriental items—make sure the stands fit exactly. In the Orient, a stand is custom-made for each specific piece. It is courting disaster to use a stand that is either too small or too large. Things topple easily off stands that are not big enough, and slide around on too-big stands. Of course an object can be fastened to the stand with the above-mentioned adhesive, and the stand likewise fastened to a table or shelf.

4. If you possess a specimen that represents a tremendous investment or is an irreplaceable rarity, keep it in an extra-safe spot. (Many of your friends may be totally unaware of the value and rarity of the things displayed in your home.)

5. If a treasure can't stand frequent dusting, washing, or cleaning, display it behind the glass doors of a cupboard or case.

6. Valuable items displayed close to a window are an invitation to thieves; but never put any objects in sunlight or close to a radiator if they will be adversely affected by strong light, excessive heat, or sudden temperature changes. Rapid swings in the temperature can cause crazing in ceramic objects, even break glass and fine china. Lacquer items warp and crack; silk deteriorates; embroidery fades.

7. Carry adequate insurance to protect your collection against fire and theft.

8. When you are away from home for overnight trips or vacations, ask a trusted neighbor to keep an eye on your home. For long absences, it is a good idea to pack away the most treasured items in a safe or fireproof and well-insulated steel trunk with a strong lock. Ultra-careful collectors keep on hand a supply of inexpensive but impressive-looking imitations to mix amongst their genuine antiques at such times. Most burglars have neither the time nor the expertise to distinguish the imitation from the genuine.

9. Keep a complete list of the items in your collection (and their value), and take color photographs of them—at least, of all the finest and most valuable specimens. Store the list and pictures in a secure place such as a safety deposit box. You will find both list and pictures invaluable if you ever need to provide proof to substantiate an insurance claim or to prove ownership if and when lost items reappear.

241. *Step one:* The base was removed so that the dented area could be pushed or hammered out; then base was replaced. Loose and broken enamel was removed and the wires were rearranged, after which the damaged area was filled with the recommended material, to a level slightly higher than the surrounding surface.

242. *Step two:* After the filler material had cured, the patch was sanded down to the desired contour. Note that the wires reappeared. The black areas are the remaining parts of the original enamel.

Repair of Cloisonné and Enamelwares

How many times is a beautiful cloisonné or enamel specimen at a cut-rate price passed up because it is damaged? The area may be only as big as a silver dollar, but with the enamel gone, the bare and discolored copper base is plainly and unpleasantly apparent. Getting it professionally repaired would cost three or four times as much as the purchase price. So most potential purchasers let such items strictly alone.

243. *Step three:* Close-up shows that the repaired area has been touched up within the wires with colors to match the original. After two thin coats of clear epoxy or plastic paint, the repair is rubbed down to the desired glossiness.

The fact is, however, that it is surprisingly easy to repair a damaged cloisonné and, for that matter, to repair many other antiques. With the various kinds of modern hobby-trade products on the market, some repairs are a downright cinch.

The basic technique is rather simple. All that is needed is to restore the damaged section so that it will look more or less like the area surrounding it—the more, the better. But of course practice makes for proficiency and perfection. Practice a lot before tackling your most treasured antiques.

There is a mistaken notion that antiques should be sold "as is," bought "as is," and should never be repaired; that repairing and restoring an antique either by the dealer or the owner smacks of dishonesty. Nothing can be further from the truth. Many of the rarest and most valuable items in museums have been repaired or restored. Large museums have repair departments staffed by the best technicians they can find. Remember, too, there is always the chance that a broken piece you are tempted to throw away may be the last of its kind.

At first you may hesitate to do the repairing yourself and prefer to engage a professional. That is certainly all right. If you have a repairman whose work always satisfies you, cherish him. If not, inquire around a bit. But don't trust just anyone who calls himself a repairman. We have seen some atrocious work done on valuable things that, in the final analysis, would have been better off left unrepaired. Before you entrust a job to a workman, examine a few samples of his work. When you are absolutely satisfied, then take your piece to him. Be sure to make clear exactly what you want him to do and what not to do because if a piece is repaired in the wrong way, it is very difficult to "disrepair" it again.

For instance, a friend of ours has a piece of beautiful porcelain that was broken in half. It is an oblong dish painted in delicate enamels, and on it is a poem composed by the emperor Ch'ien-lung and written in his handwriting. The repairman did a good job putting the two pieces together, and then he waxed creative and decided to improve the emperor's artwork with a coat of apple green glaze covering the whole dish. There never was such a style. Now our friend's treasure has become a monstrosity, or what the Chinese would scornfully refer to as "neither horse nor cow"!

Therefore, if you have a great deal of patience and are good with your hands, it is sometimes better to do it yourself. If you choose a common inexpensive piece for your first attempt, little will be lost even if you fail. Take a small piece of cloisonné for a test. Cloisonné is easily damaged. One drop or fall, and it's either cracked or dented or bashed in.

If it's bashed in, quite a bit of the glasslike enamel may be gone, and maybe even a few of the wires that form the cloisons or cells. The copper base may have been pushed in, and then you have a major repair job.

First, try gently to push the copper base out as close to its original shape as possible. Use a wooden spoon, mallet, or a stick of suitable length and shape.* In the process, more of the already cracked enamel pieces will fall out. Don't worry about them. They are no good anyway.

Then get a good filler, such as an epoxy filler or one of the other kinds of fine-grain, tough, waterproof fillers on the market. Fill in the places where the enamel is gone, building up the filler until it is just

---

* It may be necessary to remove the base plate of a cloisonné vase in order to push or hammer out the damaged part.

slightly higher than the surrounding area. As you work, try to re-arrange the wires if they are out of place.

When the filler is thoroughly dry or cured, shape it with an emery board or a piece of coarse sandpaper (240 or 280). Be sure not to let this abrasive material touch the surrounding area as you work. After the filler has been shaped to roughly the same level as the surrounding area, wash it clean and wipe it dry.

Next, with a finer sandpaper (400), continue to shape the filled-in area until it is slightly below the surrounding area. Wash and clean it again. Now switch to a still finer paper (600) and keep on polishing and smoothing it. Don't be afraid to let this fine paper touch the surrounding area. In fact, it's all right to give the whole piece a polish with a well-broken-in piece of No. 600 paper to restore its beautiful colors, which are often hidden by years of accumulated grease and grime. Wash again, and dry the whole piece with a lint-free cloth.

Set the piece before you on the table and inspect it closely. Have you restored its original contour? (That is, have you filled in the damage to just slightly below the surrounding area to allow for a slight buildup with touch-up and glazing material?) If so, the first part of the repair job is a success.

The second part is the touch-up. Get a set of fine-quality water-color paints, and paint the missing designs on the filled-in area. Designs are usually repeated over and over again on these pieces, so there should be no difficulty about finding the appropriate motif to copy. Be sure to get the colors exactly right. If any of the copper wires are missing, this is the time to paint in imitation wires. Use copper or brass paint, whichever looks most like the original wire, and trace in the missing ones. It is difficult to paint the lines very thin, but you can shape and narrow them by scraping with a razor blade. Or you can cover a too-wide part by overlapping it with watercolor paint. Inspect the piece again. If the colors and the designs match the original ones correctly, the second part of the job is a success.

The third and last part is the finishing. The original enamel was glossy or semiglossy. The repaired area is not. To give it the finished look, rub on two or three thin coats of clear epoxy glue. Do not put on thick coats because epoxy runs. Put a little on your fingertip and apply to the repaired area, covering it evenly. Wash off what remains on your finger with soap and water immediately. When the first coat is cured, put on another coat the same way. (More will be said about epoxy later.)

When the second coat is cured, you will see that you have done a good repair job. If the repaired area is glossier than you like, rub it down with a little tin oxide powder on a piece of soft cloth. If you want a still duller look, rub it gently with steel wool of the finest grade. If the result is then too dull, put on another thin coat of epoxy, wait until it is completely cured, and rub it over again—this time more gently.

Some unevenness may appear in the finishing coat because at first you may not be very good at applying the epoxy. If so, you can sand it down with a fine sandpaper. Don't sand too hard because you may remove not only the epoxy but also the watercolor paint beneath it. After sanding, apply another coat to restore the glossiness. Repeat as many times as necessary until the desired smoothness is achieved. A white sandpaper should be used; if particles from a black sandpaper become embedded in the epoxy, the repaired part will look darker.

Plastic paint can also be used as a finish coating with equally good results. Use "high gloss" or "satin finish," according to the desired glossiness.

Enamelwares are repaired in the same way, except that the work is easier because there are no wires to worry about.

Use epoxy steel to repair pewterware.

Japanese cloisonnés of the transparent enamel type are more difficult to repair. Mix epoxy glue with transparent pigment such as photo-color. The result is a kind of artificial transparent enamel. Fill in with it a little at a time until the desired buildup has been reached. This of course takes time. Each filling must be thoroughly cured before the next one is applied.

To save time, heat the mixture to hasten its curing. An ordinary heat lamp will serve the purpose nicely. You can fill in more at a time when the mixture is in a semi-cured and less runny state. Before it is completely cured, wet your finger and tap the surface gently to shape the contour. A final shaping with sandpaper is often necessary.

Mix this "artificial enamel" much lighter in color than the actual object. As each filling is applied, the color deepens. However, if the color has already become like the original before the crack or hole is filled, you can keep it from getting deeper by completing the job with colorless, clear mixture.

Two types of this imitation enamel can be made. 1. *The opaque kind:* Mix epoxy with watercolor paint. Stir the mixture constantly for two or three minutes to let the water content evaporate before using. 2. *The transparent kind:* Mix epoxy with photo-color. Do not mix in too much color—a little goes a long way.

The transparent type can also be used to fill in cracks and chips in glass items. Of course the opaque type is required to repair Peking glass. For a mixture of great opacity—for instance, for the purpose of filling in a damaged marble, soapstone, or jade—add a little white talcum powder to the mixture.

To eliminate bubbles in the mixture, spread it paper-thin on a piece of aluminum foil and blow very hard on it. When the bubbles are gone, scrape it up gently but don't stir it again.

Repair of Porcelain and Pottery

There are on the market at least half a dozen products that guarantee to glue a broken dish together in a few seconds, and when the dish is thoroughly dry in twenty-four hours, it will be waterproof and detergent-proof.

If a simple clean break is the problem, the repair is easy. But usually the collector's problems with porcelain are not that simple. A dish may be chipped all around the edge, or a vase may have a sizable piece of its neck missing. And even if a bowl is successfully glued together, the face of the beautiful lady may be partly gone because the overglaze enamel decoration along the broken line has been chipped off.

If you want such a piece repaired in a hurry and cannot wait to gain experience by working on easier pieces, don't attempt to do it yourself. We have seen repairs made with various kinds of nail polish that were a total disaster. As mentioned before, it is nearly impossible to "disrepair" a badly repaired piece. How good a job an expert repair-man can do depends on many things. If the porcelain is entirely covered by overglaze decorations, such as the mille-fleur pattern or the rose Canton type, he can and should restore it so that no damage shows. But on a mostly white piece or a monochrome of the light-colored variety, such as a clair de lune or a celadon, he will not be able to cover up the damage entirely. It's just not in the nature of things.

If you prefer to do the repair yourself, how do you proceed? First we suggest that you enroll in a hobby class to become familiar with all the wonderful modern chemical products. You will learn how to use the many substitutes for glazes and for enamel colors. You should also, if possible, take a ceramics course to become familiar with the making of pottery and the use of a kiln. If you cannot do either, you will at least be able to achieve moderate success by using the techniques we have already explained for the repairing of cloisonné and enamelwares. The main difference is that ceramic objects do break into several pieces. Often one or two may be missing, and it takes a little more time and know-how to restore such a specimen.

First of all, break a couple of common dishes that you don't care about and learn to put them together correctly. If a dish is broken into two or three pieces, you can put them together all at once. But if it is in four, five, or six pieces, don't try to glue them together in a single operation. Put just two together at a time, and be sure to mesh them precisely. Take two or three steps to finish the job. After the glue or epoxy has cured, scrape off all the excess material with a razor blade. Practice until you do a clean repair job.

Break a couple more dishes, this time chipping or breaking dime- or quarter-size pieces off the edge. Throw these chips and chunks away, and try to fill in the damaged spots. Use a white or neutral-color filler that will harden into a waterproof patch and adhere to the broken edges permanently. There are, again, many kinds of fillers on the market. A good one should be fine grained, easy to manipulate, and stand sanding after hardening. Find the one that you like to work with, and then stick to it.

After hardening or curing, sand the repaired part down to slightly below the surrounding area because, in repairing ceramics, the final coating of glaze or imitation glaze that gives the translucent look must be reasonably thick.

If a piece has a colored glaze, mix an "imitation glaze" to match the color, and then apply it directly over the repaired part. Note, however, that if the original porcelain body is very white, you may need to put a white slip over the repaired part first. A very thin coat of white watercolor paint will do.

If the item is a powder blue, do not apply the blue with a brush. First, apply a thin coat of epoxy over the repaired area. Then put some blue powder on a sheet of paper and blow it off the paper, letting it land evenly on the repaired part. Don't blow on too much at a time. Repeat several times to get the desired depth.*

If a piece has overglaze enamel decorations, success can be guaranteed. First apply a coat of "imitation glaze" over the repaired

---

* The terms "powder blue," "soufflé red," and so forth refer to a process by which the color or glaze was blown in powder form through a bamboo tube covered by gauze onto the porcelain body before firing. This method was used when the brush could not successfully make an even and uniform application.

244. Old 15-inch vase in the shape of a fisherman's basket with four crabs on the shoulder. All but three of the crabs' legs were missing, and the repair work consisted of replacing thirty-seven legs and pincers. Ca. eighteenth or early nineteenth century; Canton (Fatshan) pottery.

area. If the original glaze has a bluish or greenish cast, add a little color to make the imitation match the original. When the glaze is cured, mix the necessary "imitation enamels," and fill in the missing design. Mix one color at a time, and match the colors exactly with the original. Any piece with a complicated pattern can be touched up until not the slightest damage shows. Sometimes, it helps to add a green leaf or two, a pink rosebud, a twig, or a rock to cover up a repaired area. Since the enamels stand out from the glaze anyway, the question of overall evenness does not come up. You can literally "pile on" the imitation enamels. Remember, most oriental designs are sketched with black lines. To make the repair look authentic, don't omit these black lines.

A piece of white porcelain is the most difficult thing to repair—there are so many shades of "white." Success depends on the ability to match the exact color of the original.

A mere crack line is very hard to cover up. If the line is discolored.

245. Black lines indicate the length of the repaired area (the width is about ½″) on this Imari plate. The method of repair is fully explained in the text.

clean it as well as you can—soaking in bleach may help some, but if it is very dirty, there doesn't seem to be a really effective way to make it white again. Follow the cleaning by using white watercolor paint to cover the line, and then apply glaze over it. This naturally makes the line slightly higher than the surrounding area, so apply the glaze as thin as you can.

The steps for repairing underglaze decoration are as follows: (1) Restore the body, and cover it with a white slip if necessary; (2) paint on the necessary pattern with watercolor, either in blue or red; (3) cover with two or three coats of glaze.

To make artificial crackles, incise the finished area with a razor blade to match the crackle pattern and rub in pigment to match the color.

Repairing Lacquer

It is easy to repair any kind of lacquerware after learning how to repair cloisonné and porcelain.

First, clean the damaged area and the surrounding areas with a damp cloth. Sometimes a piece is so heavily covered with grease and grime that a little paint thinner is necessary. In extreme cases, use both paint thinner and fine steel wool. Remove loose particles.

246. *How to replace a cover*: (1) Find a cover that fits and is as close as possible to the original in color; (2) remove any unwanted decoration or design by sanding; (3) apply artificial glaze—try to match what must have been the background color of the original cover (often white, or bluish or greenish white); (4) pencil in the needed design—in this instance, the wing of the Japanese Hoo bird extends over the cover; (5) fill in the penciled design with appropriate artificial enamels; the design on this cover required blue, green, red, and yellow. (The teapot is Kutani-touzan, with Kakiemon-style decoration.)

Fill the damaged place with a filler. There are, again, many products on the market, but we feel that a paste made of spackling compound and gray outdoor latex paint serves the purpose very well. The mixture will shrink or develop some slight cracks during drying, but don't worry. Just keep filling it in until the repaired part is slightly higher than the surrounding area. Sand and shape it when dry.

247. Top of a lacquer stool of the Coromandel type. A third of the right side was completely gone, but was rebuilt and restored by using the method explained in the text. The original design had two figures holding the scroll, which bears the word "shou" or "longevity." Since it was too difficult to restore the missing figure, rocks and plants were carved as replacements. The scroll, as a result, was left flying in the wind.

If the lacquer is the carved or incised type, recarve it, using a set of carving knives you can buy at a hobby shop. For touch-up use enamel paint of different colors, and when the touch-up is dry, apply a coat or two of clear plastic paint. Use "high gloss" for glossy effect, and "satin finish" for dull effect. Sometimes it is advisable to apply two or three coats of plastic paint over the whole object, particularly one that is in none-too-good condition. This method is equal to wrapping it in an airtight plastic sack. It gives protection and keeps moisture from further damaging or weakening the piece.

Other Repairs

To repair ivory, it is necessary to use another piece of ivory and carve and/or sand it into the desired shape to replace the missing piece. Then glue it into place.

248. Teakwood tray with inlaid mother-of-pearl landscape and figures. The houses under the tree on the left side, the tree trunks, and part of the knoll on which the houses stand were replaced by using pearl buttons cut, ground, and carved to fit the original spaces exactly. The repaired section of the tray is shown in color plate 19.

To repair wood, it is always better to use the same kind of wood to replace the missing piece. Very small repairs can be made by using a little plastic wood, then staining and varnishing it to match the original.

To repair a marble top, mix epoxy glue with the desired color to match the original. The necessary degree of opacity can be achieved by mixing in the correct amount of talcum powder. Fill in the cracks and damaged areas. Sand to shape, and finally apply a coat of clear epoxy or plastic paint over the whole surface. Buff with a piece of spent sandpaper (No. 600) to restore the stone look.

A Word about Epoxy

Various kinds of epoxy products are useful in repair work. These include epoxy fillers and epoxy glues. Each type comes in two parts that are to be combined just before use. You can mix any amount you want.

Of the two, epoxy glue is the most useful to the collector who wants to make his own repairs. Its main function is to bond things together. However, the possibility of using it to make "imitation glaze" and "imitation enamels" has greatly simplified the repairing process. For these purposes, the epoxy glue must be clear and colorless. Un-

249. Trunks and tabletops were often wrapped over with calfskin (Westerners call it pigskin) and then decorated with watercolor painting frequently in the rose Canton style. The colors, however, rubbed off easily. This tabletop had no color left. Only the sketch was still visible. Repairing consisted of painting with appropriate colors over the original design, and then two coats of clear plastic paint were applied as finish.

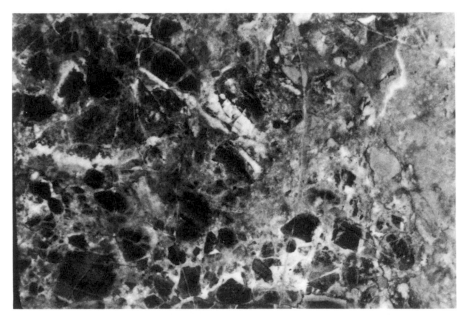

250. This marble tabletop was broken into seven or eight pieces and a lot of small chips were missing. Repairing consisted of gluing the broken pieces together with epoxy glue and filling the missing places with epoxy mixed with powder of different colors to match the original. The stone was then sanded level and two coats of clear plastic paint were applied as a finish. Because of the veins in the stone, the repaired crack lines are hardly noticeable.

fortunately, many brands are distinctly yellow after they are mixed, and this limits their use. Some brands, if mixed with colors or other substances, will not cure and harden. Others will mix with almost anything and still cure properly.

Epoxy glues are being made by many manufacturers, and you will have to try out several to learn which you prefer. We have tried nearly all brands. Strangely, the two or three kinds that are crystal clear and can be mixed with anything are made by small manufacturers.

Epoxy runs as it is curing. It usually takes from one hour to half a day to cure, depending on the brand. This means that the repair job requires constant watching—the piece must be turned frequently in different directions to prevent the epoxy from collecting at one place or running off. However, heating will greatly shorten the curing time. A heat lamp or even a 100-watt lamp placed from 12 to 18 inches away either before or after application will do the job. Learn to shape the epoxy with a finger before it hardens. First, wet your finger; then tap it on the semicured mixture. Withdraw your finger as quickly as you can—don't let it stay there or the epoxy will stick to it. Keep your finger constantly wet, as the film of water will act as a temporary insulator. We cannot tell you when you can start shaping the filler; only your own experience can tell you.

After the epoxy is completely cured, it can be sanded to shape. The cured epoxy will not be as hard as porcelain or glass—in other words, it can be easily scratched. But scratches can always be removed by rubbing on another thin coat of clear epoxy. However, it will be a lot tougher than porcelain or glass because it will not chip or break under ordinary circumstances.

APPENDIX OF MARKS*
AND PERIODS

*The term "chop marks," as used by Westerners, embraces a wide range of stamped marks. 1. *Artists' seals.* These can be the owners' sobriquets, quotations from poetry, and so on. They are often done in archaic (seal) script by prominent artists in seal-cutting. 2. *Personal seals.* Every resident in the oriental countries possesses one. The imprint it makes is as legally binding as a signature in the West. Personal seals are often in archaic script to make forgery difficult. 3. *Shop marks, manufacturers' marks, and trademarks.* These are the true "chop marks." They are always in modern script for easy reading. Besides the names and addresses of the makers or distributors, they also contain such vital information as the quality of the material and a guarantee. "Chop marks" are stamped in ink or vermilion paste. In the case of metal products, such as gold and silver jewelry, pewter, bronze, and so forth, the marks are stamped into the metal. Oriental merchants are noted for their integrity. A piece of "chop-marked" gold jewelry, for instance, is honored throughout the country, and can be instantly changed into money. People often wear one or two solid gold rings, not for the sake of ornament, but simply as an easy and sensible means of carrying an extra bit of ready cash with them.

PERIOD (5)   HUNG (3)   GREAT (1)

MADE (6)   WU (4)   MING (2)

Hung-wu (1368-1398) was the founder of the Ming Dynasty.

Chia-ching (1522-1566)

Yung-lo (1403-1424)

Lung-ch'ing (1567-1572)

Hsüan-tê (1426-1435)

Wan-li (1573-1619)

Ch'eng-hua (1465-1487)

T'ien-ch'i (1621-1627)

Hung-chih (1488-1505)

Ch'ung-chên (1628-1643)

Cheng-tê (1506-1521)

PERIOD (5)　　SHUN (3)　　GREAT (1)

MADE (6)　　CHIH (4)　　CH'ING (2)

Shun-chih (1644-1661) was the founder of the Ch'ing Dynasty.

Hsien-fêng (1851-1861)　　　　K'ang-hsi (1662-1722)

T'ung-chih (1862-1874)　　　　Yung-chêng (1723-1735)

Kuang-hsü (1875-1908)　　　　Ch'ien-lung (1736-1795)

Hsüan-t'ung (1909-1912)　　　　Chia-ch'ing (1796-1820)

Tao-kuang (1821-1850)

MARKS IN SEAL CHARACTERS

(Archaic characters)

Tao-kuang

Ch'ien-lung

T'ung-chih

Chia-ch'ing

Recent mark, which contains
simplified characters

Old mark

Recent mark

↑   ↑
Simplified characters

(Made at Ching-tê Chên, China)

Made under the supervision of Lo-sen
(Chinese mark, but made in Japan or
Hong Kong)

Made by the China Art Ceramic Company
(Taiwan)

JAPANESE MARKS

Koto

Kenya

Kutani

Eiraku

Banko

Kenzan

Kutani

Seto

Kinkousan

Kenzan

Soma

"fuku" or good luck
(mark on old wares)

Iga

Kenzan

Ninsei

Ninsei

Imari—modern

229

COMPARATIVE CHART OF HISTORICAL PERIODS

	CHINA	KOREA	JAPAN
1500	SHANG (YIN)		
1000	CHOU		
500	WARRING STATES		
0 BC / AD	HAN	LO-LANG (CHINESE COLONIES)	ARCHAIC PERIOD
100		KOGURYO, PAEKCHE, SILLA (THREE KINGDOMS)	
200			
300	PERIOD OF DIVISION		
400			
500			
600			ASUKA
700	T'ANG	SILLA	NARA
800			HEIAN
900			LATE HEIAN (FUJIWARA)
1000	SUNG	KORYŎ	
1100			
1200			KAMAKURA
1300	YUAN		
1400	MING	YI DYNASTY	MUROMACHI (ASHIKAGA)
1500			
1600			MOMOYAMA
1700	CH'ING		TOKUGAWA (EDO)
1800			
1900	REPUBLIC 1912		MEIJI

PRICE GUIDE

In providing this price guide, our intention is to give the reader a few rules or standards by which oriental objects may be evaluated. The following should not be construed as a price list. Such a list cannot be made realistically. Prices vary from dealer to dealer, and from year to year. A discussion of the market conditions with some definite examples in a broad price range may benefit the reader by helping him develop a sense of comparative values.

Chinese Bronzes

In discussing the price of bronze of the Shang and Chou periods, we can talk only in broad terms. A libation cup is worth $15,000 to $20,000; a larger vessel from $25,000 to $30,000, and an important specimen, such as a ting or p'an, with inscriptions of historical importance, is priceless.

A Han or T'ang mirror might be worth several hundred dollars. Also prized are gilded Buddhist statuettes of this period.

An incense burner of the Hsüan-tê period is priced quite high, and a good and genuine one will be worth over $1,000. However, 99.9 percent of even the very best quality with authentic-looking Hsüan-tê marks were made in a later period, and there is no foolproof way to prove authenticity.

Coming down to the eighteenth century, most good items of average size—meaning pieces a person can move around without difficulty—could be over $200, but not over $500. Inlaid items are more expensive.

For items made during the last hundred years, we can be more specific:

Incense burner of good quality and workmanship, often marked Hsüan-tê, diameter 6″ to 8″: $50–$85

Candlesticks (pair), height 16″ to 18″: $40–$60

(The above items should be heavy. Those with simpler and less involved designs are preferred.)

Export Wares

Bowls, often with dragon designs, diameter 8″ to 12″: $12–$18

Teakettles with enameled repoussé work and/or decorated with beads of glass or semiprecious stones, height 6″ to 8″: $25–$35

Iron (Chinese pressing iron), ashtrays, cigarette boxes, decorated with glass or semiprecious stones: $4–$10

Japanese Bronzes

Jars, vases, and urns using Chinese archaic motifs, some decorated with champlevé enamels and usually lacquered a deep brown color, are smooth and handsome and fairly heavy. (Height 10″ to 20″.) Those with pure Japanese forms and motifs, such as Japanese iris and storks, belong to the same price range: $50–$200.

Massive and overelaborate items, such as incense burners and urns on stands often over six feet tall, will cost around $2,000.

Ojime, tsuba, and other signed or unsigned sword furniture are expensive and for specialty collectors. There is no way to give a meaningful price range.

Korean Bronzes

Korean bronzes follow the same price range as Chinese. Archaic Korean items such as mirrors, bells, and gilded statuettes are just as rare and expensive as Chinese.

Jade

Oriental jade objects (meaning Chinese jade exclusively because, although Japan produces some jadeite, the Japanese prefer to work with wood and ivory; the cashew-nut-shaped jade beads excavated from ancient Korean tombs, the only Korean jade artifacts known, are perhaps of Chinese origin) are among the most expensive collectibles.

A six-inch-high jade incense burner with free rings on the handles would be a bargain at $1,000. A jade bracelet of white "rockish" material costs about $80. If it has one or two green spots, it will be over $100; $200 if the green spots are larger and prettier; $1,000 if the bracelet has an overall nice green color; $3,000 or more if the green is more exciting and eye-catching.

But it serves no purpose to say that a jade bracelet is worth between $80 and $3,000, depending on the quality of the stone; or that a two-inch figurine is worth between $35 and $300, depending on the quality of the jade and the workmanship; or that an archaic ritual jade of the Shang and Chou period is worth from $2,000 to $10,000, depending on its rarity and historical significance.

The quality of the material is of first importance, and quality is an elusive factor. We say a good jade must show a translucent green. But how translucent is the most desirable degree of translucence? How green is the most beautiful green? Perhaps just the right combination of translucence and shade of green is what makes a jade priceless. To describe such qualities accurately, however, is beyond the power of words. Then, too, there are the eagerly sought mutton-fat jade, the rare yellow jade, and the even rarer red jade. (Readers should be warned that coral, carnelian, and red agate are sometimes offered as red jade.)

When the raw material has several colors, the carver should have had the skill—even genius—to utilize them to the best advantage. A pure white, mutton-fat jade bowl with brown salamanders hanging over the edge reaching for a drink can be a breathtaking sight. On such a bowl, the brown skin of the boulder was cleverly exploited rather than cut away.

Good workmanship means a piece has been expertly planned and executed. The lines should be sure and unwavering, like a brushstroke. They must be deeply cut so that the relief stands out in more than one dimension. All high and low points must be well smoothed out and highly polished.

Serpentine and bowenite are often used as jade substitutes by oriental carvers, and sold as jade by Western dealers. (There are recent imports of large imitation jades carved from dyed onyx, fitted with beautiful stands and silk-lined glass-covered cases.) Most dealers, we must say in fairness, are honest, but few of them are knowledgeable about jade. They get fooled as often as their cutomers.

For an under-$100 jade piece, a scratch test is a "must." For anything much over $100, a money-back guarantee should be obtained so that the stone can be verified by a specialist.

Other Carved Stones

For carved amethyst, rose quartz, clear crystal, carnelian, agate, lapis, turquoise, and other stones, the general rule to follow is to make sure that their prices do not exceed those for identical items (meaning identical in size and workmanship) made of poor-quality jade. In rare cases, if the material is flawless, the color rich and uniform, the carving exquisite, they can still be and should be priced high.

Graphics

No one can quote a price on an early piece of Chinese art (Sung, Ming, or early Ch'ing). The same can be said of the old Korean and Japanese masters.

It is even difficult to price paintings of our contemporary age. Take, for instance, Ch'i Pai-shih. A painting of his might cost from $1,000 to $2,000. Ch'i was extremely productive, and therefore the price is reasonable. A fan or an album leaf might cost only a few hundred dollars because size traditionally has a great deal to do with the price of oriental painting. Again, one of Ch'i's works might be worth twice as much as another, simply because the one might belong to the best period of his long productive career and the other might not. Or, it could be that the master was not particularly in the mood and executed a painting perfunctorily, to order, or to fulfill a promise.

There are not many of Hsü Pei-hung's works on the market, and therefore, when a sale is consummated, it is a private matter between the seller and the buyer. Chang Ta-ch'ien has two or three studios in America. The family of the late Chang Shu-chi still retains his studio in California. Collectors can go to these studios and purchase works or find the information they want.

In the realm of commercial art, ancestor portraits made for export cost from $40 to $50. Genuine portraits should not top $100 unless the subject is a well-known or important personality.

Other types of commercial art circa 1900—genre, landscape, birds, and flowers—should run from $25 to $75.

Ceramics

Sung specimens often run into five or even six figures. (Koryŏ celadons approximate Sung porcelain prices.)

Ming classical types (Hsüan-tê underglaze blue and red, Ch'êng-hua enameled porcelain) are priced in four or five figures. Collectors are willing to pay over a thousand dollars for fine large K'ang-hsi, Yung-chêng, and Ch'ien-lung pieces.

Westerners have also raised the prices of seventeenth- to eighteenth-century export wares sky-high. Armorial porcelains are exceedingly scarce. The question is no longer how much the collector is willing to pay, but where he can find them.

The following items are more readily available:

Blue and white (Nanking or Canton type) late eighteenth- or nineteenth-century
>   Plate or bowl, diameter 6″ to 10″: $20–$75

Famille rose (rose Canton type), ca. 1900, of good-quality porcelain with good enamel decoration
>   Plates, diameter 6″ to 10″: $15–$35
>   Bowls, diameter 6″ to 12″: $20–$50
>   Vases,   8″   to   12″: $35–$65

Ch'ien-lung-style, fine, thin, compact white porcelain decorated with famille rose enamels in various favorite Chinese designs
>   Vases, 8″ to 12″: $20–$45
>   Plates, 6″ to 10″: $ 5–$25
>   Rice bowls: $ 2–$ 5

Note: Recently imports have begun to appear. The quality is as fine as in the old pieces and the prices are about the same as current antique prices. There are slight innovations in the designs, and the enamels are applied with care but very thinly.

Restaurant (chop suey) dishes
>   Serving bowls, 6″ to 10″ diameter: $5–$12
>   Serving platters, 6″   to   10″: $5–$12

Rice pattern dishes
>   Plates or saucers, 6″ to 10″: $5–$12
>   Rice bowls and/or teacups: $3 and up

Note: The blue designs on the recent imports from Japan are printed or stenciled.

Yi-hsing ware
>   Teapots of most varieties: $5–$12

Stoneware containers

>   Pickle jars, herb liquor bottles with thick glaze of
>   brown, black, white, or green, height 6″, diameter 6″: $2–$8
>   Same, height 10″ to 18″: $10–$40

Canton figurines
  Pottery and/or stoneware, height 3″ to 6″: $3–$8

Japanese Ceramics

Imari, over 100 years old
  Plates or bowls, diameter 4″ to 12″: $35–$85

Note: Those made after 1900, about 20 to 40 percent less.

Satsuma
  Vases, plates, etc.: $10–$75 (depending on size and quality)

Kutani ware
  Most was made after 1900. Prices are reasonable. The variety of items from whole sets of dishes to single objects is too great to give specific prices.

Note: Fine specimens of old Kutani, Kakiemon, Nabeshima, and Satsuma must be individually appraised.

Cloisonné, Chinese and Japanese

Vases, bowls, urns, tea jars, height 4″ to 14″: $15–$120

Matchboxes, ashtrays, salt and pepper sets, napkin rings: $5–$15

Note: Fifteenth- to eighteenth-century specimens must be appraised individually. Fine specimens of Japanese cloisonnés with exquisite decorations are priced 20 or 30 percent higher than Chinese export type.

Champlevé

Depending on the amount of decoration, champlevé costs 20 to 40 percent less than a corresponding cloisonné item.

Chinese Painted Enamels

Commercial quality painted enamels average 10 to 20 percent less than cloisonné. Fine specimens with exquisite painting must be individually appraised.

Note: Recent imports of cloisonné from China have appeared on the market. Both the quality and workmanship are good, and the prices are just about the same as for cloisonné imported before World War II. Japan is also exporting cloisonné, and again the prices are as high as on those same items exported before World War II.

Peking Glass

Snuff bottles
New: $10–$30
Old: $40–$50

Bowls
Lily bowl with scalloped or plain edges $20–$25
Heavy rice-bowl type: $40–$50
Carved bowls and deep dishes: $40–$300

Layered glass cut into geometric patterns
Vases, potpourri jars, etc.: $35–$300

Pots of free-standing trees with glass flowers, 6″ to 12″: $25–$40

Frames of flowers in various shapes and sizes: $5–$40

Miniature animals, vegetables, fruits: $1–$10

Paperweights: $4 and up

Mirror paintings (depending on the quality of the painting, framing, and size): $10–$1,000

Lantern paintings (depending on size and whether framed): $3–$20

Beads, Bangles, and Baubles

Opaque or transparent, round or elliptical, glass beads (100 to a strand): $10–$25

Lantern, tassel, or pony beads, opaque or transparent: $5–$18

Fancy beads—goldstone, mottled, overlaid, or carved (100 per strand): $20–$45

Mandarin necklace: $45–$85

Gourds, pancakes, ear drops: $2–$7

Circlets, diameter 1″ to over 5″: $0.25–$5

Chop beads (tubes): price not uniform—usually sold by the pound and depends on size, quality, and color

Costume jewelry (various types mentioned in chapter preceding): $15–$30

Cloisonné beads (Chinese or Japanese): $5–$25

Carved peach stones, Japanese ojimes, etc.: $2 and up

Chinese Lacquer

Screens (painted or incised), height 6′ to 7′, 8 to 12 panels; ca. 1900: $400–$1,000

Screens—old specimens inlaid with stones and ivory must be appraised by experts.

Tables, cabinets, commodes (painted or incised): $100–$1,000

Carved lacquer plates, bowls, vases, boxes: $15–$100

Note: New imports of good quality and workmanship from China have appeared on the market. The price is no less than for the old type.

Japanese Lacquer

Screens—old specimens and those signed by famous artists must be appraised.

Tables, cabinets: $100–$1,000

Boxes, trays, average quality: $5–$25

Note: Fine old specimens of artistic objects, including inro, must be individually appraised.

Korean Lacquer

Korean objects, except those made since the Korean War, are not often seen on the market, and must be appraised.

Ivory

A carved ivory piece should stand as a well-executed specimen of sculptural art, with skillful and detailed carving, careful smoothing of all rough corners, and an overall highly polished look. Japanese ivory figurines and other items cost as much as those made by the Chinese. They are often signed; some even carry the Chinese Ch'êng-hua (1465–1487) reign mark. Ivory netsuke, however, belong to a special field. They are sometimes sold in sets, and the collector should take pains to examine each piece individually, since the prices asked for even average-quality netsuke are by no means insignificant.

The following list represents carved items from about 1900 to World War II. It is impossible to estimate the approximate value of authentic sixteenth-, seventeenth-, and eighteenth-century pieces.

Figurines, height 3" to 10": $20–$150

Incense burners, vases (intricately carved), height 6" or more: $150 and up

Concentric, free-turning spheres with stand, 3 to 9 or more spheres: $18 and up

Card cases intricately carved, 4½" x 3" x ½": $30–$45

Snuff bottles, 2": $30–$50

Netsukes (average quality): $25–$100
(Fine specimens can run into the hundreds.)

Teakwood Objects with Carving

Nests of tables (4): $80–$200

Square tables, altar tables, arm and straight chairs (with or without mother-of-pearl inlays): $120 and up

Stools: $20–$35

Curio cabinets, 7' x 4': $350 and up

Curio stands (quality and size only considerations): $1–$75

Lanterns, height 12" to 21", with painted glass panels: $45–$85

Jewelry or handkerchief boxes (9" x 5" x 3", inlaid with shell designs): $35–$75

Serving tray with bronze decoration, 7" x 5" or larger: $10–$25

Serving tray with inlaid shell design, 7" x 5" or larger: $20–$150

Figurines, height 3" to 24"—immortals, pu-tai, water buffalo: $5–$150

Carved screens, 6, 8, or 12 panels; height 4', 6', or 8': $120 and up

Screens with porcelain tiles or black and white Tali marble (6, 8, or 12 panels; height 4', 6', or 8'): $600 and up

Camphorwood with Carving

Large trunk-size chest with overall carving: $150–$180

Large trunk-size chest with boxwood inlays: $200 and up

Chests, 3" x 3" x 3" to 12" x 7" x 6½": $5–35

Soft Wood—*Dismantled Temple and Restaurant Pieces*

Cornices and endpieces: $5 and up

Altar and doorway overhangings, 24″ to 48″: $100 and up

Chest and commode doors, sides, or tops: $20–$100

Bamboo and Rattan

Objects are so numerous and of such varied quality that a price list does not seem justified. There are imports from Hong Kong and Taiwan. Quality and workmanship are not as fine as pre-World War II items.

Textiles

The condition of any textile is of great importance. The price should be drastically reduced if the item is threadbare, moth-eaten, faded, or ready to fall apart.

K'o ssu tapestry, depending on quality, size, condition, and age: $15–$1000   (imperial robe $350–$500)

Brocade (per yard): $5–$100

Hangchow brocade scenery pictures (machine woven): $5–$25

Embroidery: no standard price

Embroidered mandarin garments: $100–$250

Rugs: no standard price

Note: Rugs from mainland China are now on the market. The price is not less than for those made just prior to World War II.

Miscellaneous Collectibles

Pewter
  Teapot, average workmanship: $15
  Candlesticks (pair), height 12″: $35 and up
  Pieces inlaid with bronze, ashtrays to large bowls: price varies according to condition

Cork Pictures
  These must be priced by size and condition and overall quality of the artwork: $5–$50

Iron Flowers (hand-wrought, depending on size): $10–$30

Dolls: $5 and up

BIBLIOGRAPHY

Beurdeley, Michel. *The Chinese Collector Through the Centuries.* Charles E. Tuttle Co., Rutland, Vermont: 1966.

Burling, Judith and Arthur. *Chinese Art.* Bonanza Books, New York: 1953.

Bushell, Raymond. *The Wonderful World of Netsuke.* Charles E Tuttle Co., Rutland, Vermont, and Tokyo, Japan: 1964.

Bushell, Stephen W. *Chinese Arts,* vols. 1 and 2. Victoria and Albert Museum, published under the authority of the Board of Education, London: 1924.

Bussagli, Mario. *Chinese Bronzes.* Paul Hamlyn, London, New York, Sydney, Toronto: 1969.

Cahill, James. *Chinese Painting.* Skira, Switzerland: 1960.

Christie, Anthony. *Chinese Mythology.* Paul Hamlyn, London, New York, Sydney, Toronto: 1968.

Cox, Warren E. *Pottery and Porcelain,* vols. 1 and 2. Crown Publishers, Inc., New York: 1944.

Erikson, Joan Mowat. *The Universal Bead.* W. W. Norton and Co., New York: 1969.

Fenollosa, Ernest F. *Epochs of Chinese and Japanese Art,* vols. 1 and 2. Dover Publications, New York: 1963.

Fry, Roger, et al. *Chinese Art.* Batsford Ltd., London, New York, Toronto, Sydney: n.d.

Garner, Sir Harry. *Chinese and Japanese Cloisonné.* Faber and Faber, London: 1954.

Goepper, Roger. *China, Korea, and Japan: The Oriental World.* Paul Hamlyn, London: 1967.

Gompertz, G. *Korean Celadon and Other Wares of the Koryŏ Period.* Thomas Yoseloff, New York: 1965.

Gorham, Hazel H. *Japanese and Oriental Ceramics.* Charles E. Tuttle Co., Rutland, Vermont, and Tokyo, Japan: 1971.

Green, David. *Understanding Pottery Glazes.* Faber and Faber, London: 1963.

Hemrich, Gerald, I. *Jade.* Gembooks, Mentone, Calif.: 1966.

Hobson, R. L. *Chinese Pottery and Porcelain.* Funk and Wagnalls, London: 1915.

————. *The Later Ceramic Wares of China.* Ernest Benn, Ltd., London: 1924.

————. *The Wares of the Ming Dynasty.* Charles E. Tuttle Co. (first edition, 1923, Benn Bros. Ltd.), Rutland, Vermont: 1962.

Honey, W. B. *The Ceramic Art of China and Other Countries of The Far East.* Faber and Faber and Hyperion Press, London: 1914.

Horizon Magazine Editors. *The History of China and the Arts of China,* 2 vols. American Heritage Publishing Co., New York: 1969.

Jenyns, Soame. *Japanese Porcelain.* Frederick A. Praeger, New York and Washington, D.C.: 1965.

————. *Later Chinese Porcelain: The Ch'ing Dynasty* (1644–1912). Faber and Faber, London: 1951.

Johnes, Raymond. *Japanese Art.* Marboro Books, by arrangement with Books for Pleasure Ltd., London, New York: 1961.

Jourdain, Margaret, and Jenyns, R. Soame. *Chinese Export Art in the 18th Century.* Spring Books, London: 1950.

Kikuchi, Sadao. *Ukiyoe.* Hoikusha Publishing Co. Ltd., Osaka, Japan: 1970.

Kondo, Ichitaro. *Toshusai Sharaku (1794–1795).* Charles E. Tuttle Co., Rutland, Vermont: 1955.

Leitch, Gordon B. *Chinese Rugs.* Dodd, Mead, and Co., New York: 1928.

McCune, Evelyn. *The Arts of Korea.* Charles E. Tuttle Co., Rutland, Vermont, and Tokyo, Japan: 1962.

National Palace Museum Illustrated Handbook. *Chinese Cultural Art Treasures.* National Palace Museum, Taipei, Taiwan: 1967.

Scott, Hugh D. *The Golden Age of Chinese Art—The Lively T'ang Dynasty.* Charles E. Tuttle Co., Rutland, Vermont, and Tokyo, Japan: 1966.

Sullivan, Michael. *Chinese Art in the 20th Century.* University of California Press, Berkeley: 1959.

————. *A Short History of Chinese Art.* Faber and Faber, London: 1962.

Swann, Peter. *An Introduction to the Arts of Japan.* Bruno Cassirer, Publishers Ltd., Oxford: 1958.

————. *Art of China, Korea, and Japan.* Frederick A. Praeger, New York and Washington, D.C.: 1963.

Tiffany Studios. *Antique Chinese Rugs.* Charles E. Tuttle Co., Tokyo, Japan: 1969.

Wills, Geoffrey. *Jade: A Collector's Guide.* A. S. Barnes and Co., South Brunswick, N.J.: 1964.

Magazines, Periodicals, Pamphlets

Carter, Marjory. "In Search of Japanese Prints." *Arts of Asia,* Mar.–
Apr. 1971.

Committee for Art at Stanford University. *Arts of the Chou Dynasty,*
Mar. 28, 1958.

Crossman, Carl L., *The Chinese Export Porcelain for the American
Market* (a design catalog). Peabody Museum, Salem, Mass.,
1964.

Gerry, Roger G., D.C., U.S.N. "Japanese Export Porcelain," *Antiques,*
June 1961.

Honey, W. B. "Early Chinese Glass." *Burlington Magazine,* Nov. 1937.

Note: The foregoing list represents a few books and periodicals readily available to readers. It does not include highly specialized or scholarly treatises for research purposes.

Index

Illustrations are indicated in italics.

A

agate, 40, 130, 233
altarpieces, bronze Chinese, *20,*
    22
amber, 40–41
    beads, 147
amethyst, 40, 233
ao-Kutani ware, 107
Arita porcelain, 102–4, *106*
Australian jade, 33
authenticity, proof of (*see also*
    specific categories), 8
auctions, 12–13

B

bamboo work, 183, *184*
    beads, 145
    prices, 239
baskets, wood, 183, 184
batiks, silk, 197–98
beads, Chinese
    amber, 147
    bone, wood, and seed, *142,*
        145, 147
    cloisonné, 145
    glass, 130–43, *140, 142*
    goldstone, 140–41, *143*
    identifying, 141
    lacquer, carved, 145
    "melon," 140
    paste, 145–47
    prices, 236–37
    Venetian style, 140–41
beads, Japanese
    bronze, 143
    carved, 143
    cloisonné, 145
    glass, 143–44
    porcelain, 144
blanc de chine, 85, *86*
blue and white ware
    Chinese, 96, *97–99, 101,* 115,
        234
    Japanese, 115–19, *119*
bone, carved, 159–60, 168–69
    beads, *142,* 169
Book of Pottery and Porcelain.
    The (Cox), 69–70
books, 199–201
bottles, glass, 131–32
    medicine ("opium"), 5–6,
        135, *136*
    snuff, 6, 7, 131, 132, 136,
        236
bottles, ivory, 161
bowenite, 232
boxwood work, *175, 180, 181,*
    182
brass jewelry, 144

brocades, Chinese, 191, 239
brocades, Japanese, 197
bronze, Chinese, 14–26, 45
    Buddhist, *16, 20, 22*
    Ch'ien-lung, 22, 25
    Ch'in dynasty, 16
    Chou dynasty, 14, *16, 22,*
        26, 121, 230
    coins, 14, *16, 20,* 25
    coin sword, *20*
    decline of, 26
    decoration, 121–23, *122*
    genuineness, determination
        of, 18–24
    Han dynasty, 16, *16, 17,* 230
    Hsia dynasty, 14
    Hsüan-tê, 22, 26
    Huang-ti, 14
    imitations, 22–24
    inlaid, *19,* 22, 121–23, *122,*
        230
    inscriptions, 15–16
    K'ang-hsi, 25
    kuei, 15 ff.
    Ming dynasty, *19,* 22, 26
    mirrors, *16, 17,* 230
    patina, 17–18, 21–24
    polishing, 18
    prices, 25, 230–31
    Shang dynasty, 14, 15, 17,
        230
    Shang-chou, 71
    Shun-chih, 25
    Sung dynasty, 25
    T'ang dynasty, 230
    Three Kingdoms, *20*
    ting, 15 ff.
    vessels, 15–26
    weapons, 14–15, *20*
bronze, Japanese, 26–27
    beads, 143
    decoration, *26,* 27, *28–30,*
        125
    enameled repoussé (export
        ware), *23*
    inscriptions, 24
    Modern, *23, 26*
    motifs, Chinese, *23*–25, *24;*
        Japanese, *23*
    prices, 26, 231
    pseudoarchaic Chinese, *23–*
        25, 24
    standards, 26
bronze, Korean, 26–27, 231
Buddhism, Chinese
    bronzes, *16, 20,* 22, 230
    lacquer, 149
    painting, 51, 52, 53, 66, 67
Bun-gin-ga painting, 57
Burma jade, 33, 40

Bushell, Stephen W., *86*
buying antiques. *See also*
    specific categories
    advertised items, 13
    auctions, 12–13
    cautions, 5–8
    certificates and proof of
        authenticity, 8
    flea markets, 10–11
    garage sales, etc., 12
    prices, 8, 9–13. *See also*
        Prices
    shops, 9–10
    shows, 13
    thrift shops, 11–12

C

calfskin, repair, *221*
calligraphy, Chinese, 45, *49,*
    49–50, *50*
    books, 201
    Han dynasty, 51
    ink stick, inkstone, and
        brushes, 202
    Sung dynasty, 49, 52
    T'ang dynasty, 49
    Wei dynasty, 49
camphorwood carvings, 176–
    82, *180,* 238–39
Canton
    pottery, *88–91, 94–96, 95*
    stoneware, 76
care and repair, 156, 208–23
    calfskin, *221*
    cloisonné and enamelware,
        210, 210–15, *211*
    epoxy glues, 221–23
    gold paint, 181–82
    ivory, 221
    lacquer, 218–20, *219*
    lacquer, imitation, 154–56
    marble, *222*
    porcelain and pottery, 208–
        9, 215–18, *217, 218*
    silk, embroidered and deco-
        rated, 192
    teakwood, 209, *220, 221*
carnelian, 40, 233
Castiglione, Giuseppi (Lang
    Shih-ning), 46, *46–49*
cautions for collectors, 5–8
celadon, Chinese, 75–76, 77.
    See also Porcelain
celadon, Japanese, *108*
celadon, Korean, 79, *79,* 233
Ceramic Art of China and
    Other Countries of the
    Far East, The (Honey).
    70

243